CHRIST, MUHAMMAD AND I

Mohammad Al Ghazoli

Translated by R. Winston Mazakis
Edited and Annotated by David W. Daniels

CHICK
Publications
Ontario, Calif 91761

For a complete list of distributors near you,
call (909) 987-0771, or visit **www.chick.com**

Copyright © 2007 Mohammad Al Ghazoli

Published by:
CHICK PUBLICATIONS
PO Box 3500, Ontario, Calif. 91761-1019 USA
Tel: (909) 987-0771
Fax: (909) 941-8128
Web: www.chick.com
Email: postmaster@chick.com
Printed in the United States of America

ISBN: 978-0-7589-0142-2

Editor's Note:

The Arabic names of the Suras (meaning books, or chapters of the Qur'an) are the same in all translations. But the numbering of verses varies between them. I have used the numbering found in Yusuf Ali's translation. Other translations may vary by one or two verses. If you do not find what you are looking for, check the verses before or after the number given in this book.

This book is a revision of the original Arabic work written by Mohammad Al Ghazoli and translated into English by Dr. R. Winston Mazakis, President of The Middle East Mission, Inc. Ghazoli's work (and Mazakis' translation) sometimes bring out meanings of the Arabic in the Qur'an and Hadith (plural: *Ahadith*) that are not evident in a single English translation. Muslims believe there is no single authoritative translation of the Qur'an; they call all translations "interpretations." Except where noted, the verses are written in Yusuf Ali's translation.

I have added extra references that confirm Ghazoli's many sources, from the Qur'an,[1] *Hadith, Sunnah*[2] and other writings, to further document his important research. I have also added annotations that clarify information that many or most Muslims know, but few others.

– David W. Daniels

---

1) Four main translations of the Qur'an may be found at:
www.sacred-texts.com/isl/htq/index.htm
2) Various Hadith and Sunnah writings may be found at:
www.usc.edu/dept/MSA/fundamentals/hadithsunnah/

Contents

To my two sisters
To my little church south of Chicago
To the memory of my father who died as a Muslim
To all Muslims on this earth
To all those who are lost and wandering
I present this humble effort.

Introduction

The "I"

As Muslim friends and relatives say: "God save us from the word 'I'." I do not use this "I" with pride and arrogance. God forbid! Allow me therefore to use now the word 'I' in this introduction.

I am a man who lost his way for more than forty years.

I am someone who drowned himself in absolute ignorance, wondering aimlessly, and in sin... In the meantime, I was a little infant who looked up towards heaven – that heaven that has the meaning of eternity.

I am an infant who asked himself, before asking others, about the meaning of existence, birth and death.

I am someone who walked on the long road, searching for the truth in all the corners and on all roads.

I am someone who asked this world and history about Moses, Jesus and Muhammad.

I am someone who finally recognized that I was a captive in the dungeon of vanity in the huge prison whose name is the unreasoning in the world of religion.

I am someone who finished his university studies, received his master's degree in economics and political science in Egypt.

I am someone who began his business life by managing

the editor's office of an Arabic newspaper. Two years later, I became the editor-in-chief.

I worked for five years as the press counselor to an Arab president.[3]

I have published, in Arabic and international markets, tens of books, on economics, sociology, and politics. Some have been translated into three languages.

I am someone who wrote over 2000 articles that were published in Arabic and Islamic newspapers and magazines. Those articles and that research have been the resources for many Arabic and international press agencies.[4]

I met with Arab and Muslim kings and presidents without exception during the eighties and the nineties.

I am someone who criticized the Torah and the Gospel in more than one lecture and research, and repeated as a parrot that the Bible has been tampered with and changed.

I am someone at whose door a brother knocked and said, "Have you read the Qur'an and Muhammad's sayings (*Al-Hadith*) in depth?" After reading, I was stricken with a severe intellectual headache that resulted in writing my last book, *Lost between Reason and Faith* (published in Arabic only). Consequently, I found myself outside the borders of religion for more than ten years. During that time I was only looking up to heaven because I was always convinced that heaven has a Lord.

While I was lost as far as the Islamic religion is concerned, a born-again Christian put a Bible in my hands, and said "Read," exactly as it is reported that a spirit posing as the angel "Gabriel" said to Muhammad in the desert of Ghara'.

---

3) Mu'ammar al-Qadhafi
4) See chart at end of Introduction.

I read, and behold the clouds dissipated, and the sun came out in my life. The meeting was precious between this lost, wandering bond-slave and the Lord Jesus Christ.

How did I come to know Jesus Christ as my Saviour and Redeemer? Meeting Him was not a coincidence, for I have walked for a long time on the road of thorns; but my walk and my wrestling with the devil was longer. Let me tell my story briefly; for this book is not about my personal life, but rather is a candle intended to light the way before those who live in darkness.

Allah the Misleader?

When I was in the seventh grade, our religion teacher, Mahmood Qasem, said "Allah guides whoever he wants" and "Allah prospers whoever he wants without measure." He used to wear a red fez on his head (even though it was no longer fashionable by the end of the 1950s). He was gentle and courteous, but that red fez was a problem. It made the students mock and play practical jokes on him. I had an excellent relationship with him. Unfortunately, it did not last long, because one day he said in class:

"Allah prospers whoever he wants without measure."

Then he contradicted himself by quoting another verse:

"*Seek diligently* in the lowest places, and eat of his provisions, for unto Him is the final decision."

Other verses of the Qur'an say that Allah misleads whom he pleases.[5] One of those verses attracted my attention and I asked the teacher:

"How can Allah guide whoever he wants and mislead whoever he wants? If guiding and misleading

---

5) These suras in the Qur'an clearly say that Allah misleads (leads astray) people whenever he chooses: 4:88; 6:39; 13:27; 14:4; 16:93 and 74:31.

are in the hands of Allah, why then should there be a judgment and a punishment? Isn't Allah unjust if he guides and misleads as he wants?" (The idea is that Allah is not satisfied just by guiding some, but he also misleads anyone he wants.) I asked my teacher, "Is one of Allah's attributes, The Misleader?"

He was surprised at my question. It seemed that my teacher was incapable of giving an answer. He said:

"This subject needs detailed explanation, and I did not expect from a child at your age to ask me such a question. I will give you the answer; but I will need enough time."

Weeks passed without an answer. I began to think the subject had found its way into oblivion because he could not find a convincing response.

About four months later my teacher recited something similar to what happened earlier, containing similar contradictions. He said at the beginning of the lesson:

"Seek diligently in the lowest places and eat of his provisions, for unto him is the final decision."

Then at the end, he said in his holy book:

"Allah prospers whoever he wants without measure."

I compared the two statements. The first statement tells us that man had to *seek and labor for his livelihood*, but at the end of his lecture, he told us that it was *Allah who gives regardless of what man does*, for he has the final decision. At the end of his lecture, the teacher said:

"There is no need to labor and seek for your livelihood, because the decision for your livelihood and the promise thereof are in heaven (in the hand of Allah). Therefore, prosperity here does not depend

on labor and diligence, but is a decision of Allah. He
can give or not give; he can give without measure."

I felt it necessary to return to the topic with my teacher.

"Was there any logic or justice in that? How could
Allah give to those who do not work, and not give to
those who do work?"

He said he would answer me later, but again he did not.
However, this time, he called my father and told him:

"Your son asks too many sensitive questions and
questions much bigger than his age."

My father asked me what I had asked the teacher, and
after a short time, he said: "May Allah guide you my son."

I answered:

"Dad, there is a verse in the Qur'an that says Allah
guides whoever he wants and he misleads whoever
he wants. I believe that I am one of those who were
misled by Allah."

That was the beginning of my doubts. Doubts continued,
but in the traffic-jam of my business life I attempted to forget. Yet down deep I had too many questions that needed
answers. Because of that, eighteen years ago I began to re-
read the Qur'an and the Hadith (traditions of Muhammad
and his companions). I also studied in depth the deeds of
Muhammad and his successors.

As I read much on that subject, the picture slowly became clear. I became positive, in a moment of calm, that
the Qur'an is a *man*-made book and Muhammad was *not* a
messenger of God. But I kept my findings a secret. For years
I wondered about my many questions. Was faith in the conscience or in the mind? Was the truth in God without His
messenger? But where were the teachings of God?

At this time, when I reached the zenith of my vocational and financial glory, where the sales of my books reached the seven-digit figure, I found myself wrestling within, and Satan began his war against me. My relation with religion had ended and I had no ties with Islam, other than living in a Muslim society. I was in a hard situation. I realized that Islam was not the Truth and could not be the Truth. But where was the Truth?

Fear from the Fearful

After reading in-depth the Qur'an and Muhammad's Hadith and deeds, a strange picture about Islam was formed in my head. How could Muhammad control the minds of more than one billion people in this world? Can't they reason? Don't they read?

"Fear from the fearful" is a principle formulated by Muhammad, *to rule and to control the hearts of men through fear.* But what does this principle show? I can only ascertain that Muhammad, the son of Abd Allah, was one of the greatest geniuses of history. The proof for this is the millions of people marching behind him and living by his teachings. He used his natural intelligence to formulate a simple yet cunning principle.

After the death of his first wife, Khadija, who left him a great inheritance, he found the first nucleus of followers. They were slaves, poor men and those who had an interest in succeeding him, such as Abu Bakr and 'Uthman ibn 'Affan – both very well-to-do merchants, who had dealings with Khadija the wife of Muhammad before her death.

When things became difficult for him in Mecca, he fled to Medina with thirty men. While there, the number of his followers doubled to sixty. But here, Muhammad's challenge became obvious. Where would he get enough money to meet their expenses? Where would he get the money to spend on the houses he opened after the death of Khadija, marrying two women and opening two houses? Within about six months of his arrival in Medina, his houses grew to five.

Muhammad decided to use those men to raid the tribes and caravans going from Damascus to Mecca. He raided caravans, killing anyone who resisted him. Muhammad's repeated raids became the easiest means to get the needed funds. And the more funds that were available, the more men joined his gang.

Soon he was not satisfied with simple caravan raids, so he began raiding larger tribes and villages, then some towns and cities. He distributed to his men the wealth that was looted, as well as the slaves and the women. *There were no restrictions on torturing and killing captives.*

Within only three years, Muhammad formed an army of over six thousand fighting followers. As things developed, his organization was not limited to raiding caravans and villages within the Arabian Peninsula, but extended into planning invasions of other countries.

Muhammad's influence became strong, and the number of his wives rose to eleven, plus six harems of women with whom he had intercourse. It is said he had about two hundred servants and maids. The only duty of one (Abd Allah bin Mas'oud) was to take care of his shoes. He acquired enough wealth to form an army.

Muhammad had to secure his position, so "Gabriel" came down carrying the needed verses from Muhammad's god Allah, saying that *whoever would leave Islam should have his blood spilled* (Sura 4:89). Here is the verse that came down as his absolute protection and gave him all the rights he wanted and eliminated all obligations:

"So take what the Messenger assigns to you, and deny
yourselves that which he withholds from you."[6]

Muhammad was assured that *whoever embraced Islam and
then thought of leaving it, would die.* In the meantime, Allah
ordered Muslims to obey all Muhammad's commands without question. *Everyone was scared… but everyone had the duty
to kill any fearful Muslim who tried to leave Islam.*

Also by Allah's order, Muhammad was allowed to get
married without witnesses, in contradiction to the Islamic
rules he preached. He became a prophet upon whom no
laws were enforceable, even though he confessed that he was
just a human. He reached the stage where he could order to
them to kill, and they killed; and by his orders they cut the
hands and legs off the captives, even buried them alive. And
"Gabriel" carried down all the needed verses that made it
legal for Muhammad to do all that he thought necessary.

Muhammad planted the philosophy of "fear from the
fearful" in the heart of his scared followers. The Muslims
multiplied, but leaving meant certain death, even at the
hands of his closest relatives and friends. Otherwise they
would be completely shamed.

Muhammad gave his men the right to marry up to four
wives. Birth control in Islam has always been illegal. Consequently, their numbers increased. Most were Muslims by
inheritance, and they continued in their religion because of
fear. But we are not living in the age of "the rod for the dis-
obedient." We are living in the age of democracy, civil liberty,
freedom of opinion and speech and the choice of faith.

Because of this, many of the fearful began to liberate
themselves from their fear and revolt against Muhammad

---

6) Sura 59:7

and his teachings. Their number is still small, but we are living in the age of knowledge, and the Internet is doing its job in the propagation of the truth and is meeting the need of men to know. Now I am inviting the Muslims to:

"Come to the True God. Come to Jesus Christ, without fear, for He takes care of His children."

Many people warned me against making my faith public. But my answer has always been: I deal with the True God whose name is Jesus Christ, and the Bible assures me:

"Surely He shall deliver thee from the snare of the fowlers, and from the noisome pestilence. He shall cover thee with His feathers, and under His wings shalt thou trust. His truth shall be thy shield and buckler. Thou shall not be afraid for the terror by night, nor for the arrow that flieth at noonday."[7]

The Meeting

After staying a long time as an unconcerned Muslim, outside the religion of Muhammad, Satan became sure that I would not go back to the religion of Muhammad. He began his secret and public war against me, to rob me of my wealth first, then to destroy every thing I had built through the years. He appeared to me at night in the form of three angels with the same countenance. Sometimes long discussions ensued, and after they left, I found presents around the house, or money I did not have in my billfold. But when these 'angels' realized I would never go back into Muhammad's fold, they attacked my health to the point that I came close to death. I spent most of my time in hospitals. Soon I lost both my money and my prestige.

In the midst of my disaster, a lady called on the phone,

_____

7) Psalm 91:3-5

saying "I would like to see you." I really did not care to respond. But she called again, and this time I decided to see her, even though I was exhausted and my body was sick. When I met her, she placed a Bible in my hands. I opened it haphazardly, and the first thing that popped up before my eyes was the following verse:

"Come unto me, all ye that labor and are heavy laden, and I will give you rest."[8]

What is this? What am I reading? I could not sleep. My "night visitors" ceased to come. My health got worse. In the meantime, I was reading the Bible. I could not understand certain phrases I was not accustomed to reading. Those were words that could only come from the True God ("Love your enemies… bless them that curse you").

I continued reading. Why had I never seen this book, when I had read hundreds of books?

"Pray for them who despitefully use you, and persecute you… do good to them that hate you."[9]

These wonderful words could not come except from a great God who heals the sick and raises the dead. What a Lord! What a beloved Jesus, who said:

"I am the way, the truth and the life!"[10]

Yes, He is the way, and I surrendered my soul to the Lord Jesus Christ, and behold, everything changed. Things gradually returned to normal. It seemed as though I entered a different valley… a green, wonderful valley. How beautiful it is for the soul to surrender to its God and Lord, Jesus Christ. You will feel real joy, peace and love.

---

8) Matthew 11:28
9) Matthew 5:44-45
10) John 14:6

Now I live in the hands of my Lord, hoping that my people and my family, who are Muslims, will come to know the Truth, as I did, because I wish them real joy in this life and in the hereafter.

I was not satisfied with only meeting my Lord, praising His name and praying to Him. It is my obligation towards my family and my people to present to them the Truth in the words of this book, ***Christ, Muhammad, and I.***

Please read it, for in it you will find healing for your soul, and learn how you can return to the True God. I invite you to read, understand and compare. May God bless you.

Education:
• 1952-1960: El-Zaqaziq Primary and Intermediate School.
• 1960-1964: El-Saidia Secondary School, Giza, Egypt.
• 1964-1968: College of Economical and Political Sciences, Ain Shams University, Cairo, Egypt.
• 1973: Benghazi University. Libya. Master in Economics. Thesis: "The Historical Evolution of the Economics of the Arab World."

Employment:
• 1969: Literary Editor, *Balagh* (Truth) Newspaper, Libya.
• 1970: Managing Editor, *Balagh* Newspaper, Libya.
• 1970: Chief Editor, *Balagh* Newspaper, Libya.
• 1970-1974: Information Consultant to President Mu'ammar al-Qadhafi, Libya.
• 1975: Economic Consultant to the Arab League, Cairo.

• 1981: Chief Editor, *El-Arab* International magazine.
• 1979-1990: Chief Executive Officer, Arab Publishing
House, Cairo.

Publications: (all written in Arabic):
• *Libya between Two Eras.* (Tripoli, Libya: Al-Morabiteen
Publishing House, 1972).
• *Libya and Al-Aqeed and September.* (Benghazi, Libya: The
Truth Press, 1975).
• *The Free Economy: Kuwait.* (1978, Moselhy Press, Cairo).
• *Al-Saudia: Yesterday's Desert…Today's Petroleum* (1979,
Tuhama Publishing).
• *The Jordanian Economy: Where Is It Going?* (1982).
• *The Arabian Gulf: Progressive Economy.* (1986).
• *Terrorism.* (International Ideas House, 1999).
• *Lost between Reason and Faith.* (Jordan: Arabian
Publishing House, 1987).
• *Christ, Mohammad and I.* (2003) (Arabic original).
• More than 2,000 Articles published in Arabic
Newspapers, 1969 – 1998.

1

Allah's Messenger or a Man with a Message?

In this chapter we will discuss the personal life of Muhammad, the prophet of the Muslims and messenger of Allah. You will see both his personal life and his deeds before he became a "prophet of Allah." Then we can answer these important questions: Was Muhammad really Allah's Messenger to men? Did his deeds confirm his prophethood? Or did they do the opposite? You will soon find out.

Who was Muhammad?

Muhammad was the son of ("*Ben*") Abd Allah bin Abd Al-Muttalib, bin Hisham, bin Abd Munaf, bin Qusai, bin Kilab, bin Murra, bin Ka'b, bin Lu'ayy, bin Ghalib, bin Fahd, bin Malek, bin Al-Nadr, bin Kinana, bin Khuzaima, bin Mudraka, bin Elias, bin Mudar, bin Nizar, bin Ma'ad, bin 'Adnan. It is said that 'Adnan was one of the children of Ishmael, but this is not confirmed by Muslim scholars. No writer on the life of Muhammad ever mentioned 'Adnan as a son of Ishmael. Further, the Bible does not mention him among Ishmael's children. What is of interest here is the fact that Muhammad's roots were *Jewish* roots, because Mudraka bin Elias bin Mudar was a Jew from the tribe of Gad.

Muhammad was born in 570 AD, in the Arabic "year of the elephant." At the time of his birth his father Abd Allah was already dead. His grandfather, in depression over his son's death, called his grandson "Kutum," a word derived from an Arabic verb that means "to keep a secret" or "dimness" or "gloom." Later in life he met the priest bin Sa'ida, who called him "Ahmed." Later, still another priest, Buheira, altered his name to the one the world uses, "Muhammad."[11]

When Muhammad was only eight years old, his grandfather and guardian, Abd Al-Muttalib, died. Muhammad was handed over to his Uncle Abu Talib.

[It will be good here to tell a story that is widespread among Muslims. Muhammad's father, Abd Allah, was also known as "Al-Zabih," meaning "the sacrifice." The story tells us that his father, Abd Al-Muttalib, saw in a dream where some lost artifacts were buried. He followed those directions and dug in the place that he saw in his dream, and he found the long-buried Zamzam water fountain.[12] He also found some swords, garments, and a golden gazelle that he displayed by the Ka'aba.

At that time Abu Talib had only one son, Al-Harith. There, he was warned that if he had ten children, he should offer one of them as a sacrifice. The day came when ten children were born to him, so he told them of the warning and they conceded. He gave forth the lot, and the lot fell on Abd Allah. Because he loved Abd Allah, his youngest, he decided

---

11) Recorded by Al-Tabari and Imam As-Suheili, widely considered to be great Muslim scholars.
12) See also *Muhammad: His Life Based on the Earliest Sources* by Martin Lings (Rochester, VT: Inner Traditions, International, 1983), pp. 1-11.

to have a second round in giving forth the lot. And again, it fell on Abd Allah. The Third lot also fell on Abd Allah. So, Abd Al-Muttalib took his sword and intended to slay his son, but his people of Quraish stopped him. Instead of Abd Allah, he slew one hundred camels.]

After the death of Muhammad's grandfather, his uncle, Abu Talib, became his guardian. Muhammad was under his uncle's guardianship from the age of eight to twenty-five. Then he married Khadija. Abu Talib lived until the tenth year of Muhammad's calling. He and his children were Muhammad's greatest backers. But we must ask why Muhammad's uncle Abu Talib supported Muhammad when he didn't really believe in the Islamic faith, even at his death?

Muhammad Abd Al-Wahab, a scholar of Islam, wrote:

"But he refused to embrace the religion of Muhammad, fearing shame."[13]

When death came to Abu Talib, Muhammad entered his room, where were Abu Jahl and Abd Allah bin Umia, and he said: "Uncle, say, 'There is no God but Allah and Muhammad is the Messenger of Allah.'" He answered him from his death bed, "I am of the religion of Abd Al-Muttalib (his father)." He refused to respond to Muhammad's invitation to embrace Islam.

Was his uncle a Jew, a Christian, or a heathen? Some scholars say he was a pagan who believed in Manat and Uzza, goddesses of Mecca. Others say he was a Christian who believed in Christ and the Bible, and the proof of that, his statement: "The best of men know that Kutum (Muhammad) is the minister of Moses and of Christ the son of Mary." Even though he made that famous statement, Abu

---

13) See *The Life of the Messenger* by Imam Muhammad bin Abd Al-Wahab.

Talib refused to recognize Muhammad as a prophet and continued to call him Kutum.

Abu Jahl was Muhammad's second uncle, known as Abu Al-Hakam[14], who was very well learned in Mecca, and he possessed the greatest library in the Arabian Peninsula. He was a teacher of philosophy and religious studies. He was a Christian[15] with strong faith in his beliefs. He said:

> "If Muhammad had moral strength, he would say Christ is the Truth."

Another famous saying of his is:

> "The priest ceases to be one when he misleads people, because the priest is supposed to guide people not to mislead them."

In that statement, he meant the priest bin Sa'da who adopted the calling of Muhammad, along with the priest Waraqa Ibn Nawfal, who laid the foundation upon which Muhammad built his calling. Abu Hakam was one of the most educated people in Arabia, but he refused to accept the calling of his nephew. He did not only reject that calling, but he fought it, and he made this famous statement: "Their Torah is our Torah, and our Gospel is their book."

At that time, Mecca's society was composed of three coexisting branches, paganism, Judaism and Christianity. However, a big majority of Mecca was Jewish. But Christianity dominated the edges of Arabia, such as Yemen and Oman, where there were many monasteries and churches. So many of the Arabian traders who visited those areas accepted Christianity and spread it throughout the peninsula.

---

14) Also known as 'Amr bin Hisham. See also Chapter 3.
15) People and movements labeled "Christian" in this book are usually referring to a ritualistic religion with roots in Catholicism.

Muhammad's Quraish tribe in Mecca was mainly pagan with some Christians. But Muhammad's own family, members such as Abu Talib, Abu Al-Hakam and Abd Al-Muttalib, were mainly Christian.

Abu Talib was a poor man who received no help from his well-to-do brothers. Muhammad worked as a shepherd when he was a young man. At the age of twelve, his uncle took him to Damascus. During that trip, Priest Buheira met him. He asked him to come back, because Buheira liked to hear the Arabians recite the memorized poetry they were famous for. Muhammad was no good at memorizing poetry, but at least he could recite rhyming prose.

Muhammad reached age twenty-five, and was still not married, although the average age for young men to marry was eighteen. When a man reached his twenties without getting married, he usually came under a big question mark! Why did Muhammad not marry until he was twenty-five?

As we mentioned, Muhammad's uncle was poor. In the meantime, Muhammad did not have any possessions to help him get married. For this reason, Muhammad could not get married until a forty year old lady came along, with much wealth. Her name was Khadija bint Khuwaylid, a Christian widow who inherited the great wealth of her husband. So Muhammad was happy to marry her because he finally found a house to live in with a wife who was as old as his own mother. At that wedding, Abu Talib, his uncle made his famous statement:

> "Praises be to Allah who has rid us of worrying and distress."[16]

Muhammad was married after the Christian rites in one

---

[16] From *Al-Sira Al-Halabia* by Burhan El-Deen Al-Halabi.

of Mecca's convents. He never dared to marry another woman while Khadija was still alive, even though she was seventy at her death (while he was only fifty-three). However, serious frustrations emerged in Muhammad after the death of his first wife Khadija, to the point that he married two young women in one night: Aisha who was nine-years-old and Sawda bint Zam'a who was twenty-seven.

The Calling of Muhammad

When did his revelation begin? How could Muhammad know that he was an expected prophet? Who told him that he was the Messenger of Allah to that nation? We will quote Muslim scholars. Al-Halabi wrote:

> "Muhammad was afraid that the one who was bringing down the revelation to him was a demon, but Khadija assured him saying, Satan does not have any control on you."[17]

Malek bin Nabi said:

> "The prophet used to reveal his anxieties to his compassionate wife, and to complain to her that he thought he was touched by insanity that was caused by some evil witchcraft; Khadija reassured him, saying, Allah will not confound you, but you will strengthen the weak."[18]

Al-Suyuti[19] recorded:

---

17) *Al-Sira Al-Halabia* by Al-Halabi, p. 380. See also the *Hadith* of Sahih Muslim & *The Life of Muhammad* by Dr. Muhammad Hussein Haikal (1982), pp. 148-149.

18) *The Second Phenomenon* by Malek bin Nabi, p. 140.

19) Imam Abu al-Fadl 'Abd al-Rahman ibn Abi Bakr Jalal al-Din al-Suyuti (1445-1505) was an almost encyclopedic Egyptian teacher and author of almost 500 works, one of the most prolific Muslim writers. He is commonly known as "Al-Suyuti."

"Muhammad was afraid that the one who was appearing to him in the desert was a demon, and he could not believe it was an angel of God, for this reason, he used to be clad by fear and terror; his body would tremble and his color would change. He would say to Khadija, I am afraid of the demons for my life, but she would reassure him, saying, You are not one who can be touched by the devil."[20]

Studying those records about Muhammad's calling raises some serious questions. Could not that revelation carrier come down to Muhammad without causing him all that trouble? Could not that angel convince Muhammad that he was God's Messenger? Was he incapable of convincing Muhammad of his calling? Could Muhammad's wife know more about Muhammad's calling than him? Could Muhammad's wife be more convincing than the angel himself, who was the messenger? Could not that angel wipe the doubt from his mind, especially in those times when he thought the angel was a demon? Should not the angel himself have easily proved that he was an angel of God, if he really was?

One last question: How could Muhammad and Khadija finally make sure Muhammad was one of the prophets?

Dr. Sa'id 'Ashur stated:

"When Khadija uncovered her head and her chest, (in the presence of the one who was bringing the revelation) he was embarrassed and so he disappeared. Therefore, he was an angel, not a demon."[21]

Ibn Hisham wrote:

"Khadija said to Muhammad, Can you tell me

---

20) *The Jurisprudence of the Life of Muhammad* by Al-Suyuti, pp. 68-69.
21) *The Jurisprudence of the Life of Muhammad* by Dr. Sa'id 'Ashur, pp. 28-29.

whenever your friend that visits you, comes. He answered, Yes. When he came, he told her. So, she said to Muhammad, Get up and sit on my left thigh. He did. She said, Do you see him now? He answered, Yes. She said, turn and sit on my right thigh. He did. She asked him, do you still see him? He answered, Yes. She was disappointed and she took her cover and threw it down, while the Messenger of Allah (Muhammad) was sitting on her lap; she said to him: Do you still see him? And he answered her, No. She said to him: Be sure and rejoice, by Allah, he is an angel and not a demon, because demons do not get embarrassed (and disappear when women uncover), but the angels do."[22]

This story was reported in many Islamic references.[23]

This was Khadija's test to make sure Muhammad was a prophet and that phantom was an angel, not a demon. But why don't other prophets need reassurances concerning God's revelation? And why was that story needed to confirm Muhammad's calling? Could not God convey the needed knowledge about his prophet without all those fables?

That angel — or demon — was not satisfied by appearing to Muhammad and telling him what he needed to know. He also attempted to squeeze his neck and choke him almost to death. That was at the beginning of Muhammad's revelation. Later, whenever the angel came to him, Muhammad used to suffer a nervous attack, and he even passed out:

22) *The Life of the Prophet* by Ibn Hisham, p. 174.
23) See *The Beginning and the End* by Ismail Ibn Kathir, Vol. III, p. 15; *Sirat Al-Maghazi*, by Ibn Ishaq, p. 133; *Rawd Al-Unuf* by Ibn Hisham, pp. 271-272; *The Life of Muhammad* by Dr. Haikal (1982), p. 152; and *Al-Isaba fi tamyiz al-Sahaba (Finding the Truth in Judging the* [Muhammad's] *Companions)* by Ibn Hajar Asqalani (1372-1449), Vol. IV, p. 273.

"Ibn Ishaq said, the Messenger of Allah (Muhammad) said, 'Gabriel' came to me and said, Read. I answered, I am not a reader (I am not about to read). He choked me until I thought I was dying. Then he let go. He said again, Read. I said to him, I am not a reader. He choked me again until I thought I was dying. Then he let go. He said to me for the third time, Read. I said, What shall I read? He choked me until I thought I was dying, then he said, Read in the name of thy Lord...."[24]

I do not comprehend the meaning of this story. Was "Gabriel" not recognized, that he needed to violently ask Muhammad the same question three times? Why did he have to choke him almost to death, three times? He choked him when he was not about to read, and he choked him when he was about to read. Why? Could not God convey to His prophet the needed message without all that dramatic effort? That story raised many questions and many doubts.

Al-Halabi recorded:

"Whenever (parts of) the Qur'an came down upon Muhammad, he would pass out after he trembled and shuddered. His eyes closed and his face was dreary, and he would snore like a camel. Those things happened to him before the revelation came down upon him. They also tried to protect him from the spell of evil eyes."[25]

He also reported:

"At the time of the coming down of the revelation upon him, Muhammad's forehead would drip with sweat, even in cold days; and his eyes became red

24) *The Life of the Prophet* by Ibn Hisham, Vol. I, p. 173.
25) *Al-Sira Al-Halabia* by Al-Halabi, p. 407.

and wither like a drunk man. Muhammad used to say, Every time I received the revelation, I thought I was going to die."[26]

Any physician would confirm that those were the signs of epilepsy. Why did the prophet of Allah have an epileptic fit while a revelation came down upon him? The opposite should have happened at every appearance... peace, joy, assurance, and trust. Could we learn about the true nature of "Gabriel," the angel of peace, by all the awful things Muhammad experienced?

Too many questions may be raised in the mind of the reader, and I am sure that the answers will be painful ... because the truth is painful. I say "painful" because Muhammad himself said Satan often came to him in the form of "Gabriel." This fact was confirmed by Al-Halabi:

"Some interpreters mentioned that Muhammad had an enemy among the demons called the White, and he used to come to him in the form of "Gabriel.""[27]

The well-known book, *The Spirit of the Islamic Religion*, says Muhammad used to realize the difference between Satan and "Gabriel."[28] But the proof is in this Qur'an verse, where he praised the idols of Quraish as great gods:

"Those supreme idols whose advocacy should be sought."[29] The idols that are meant here were Al-Lat, Al-Uzza and Manat, the gods of Quraish. Al-Suyuti says that Satan was the one who put in

---

26) *Al-Sira Al-Halabia*, p. 115.

27) *Al-Sira Al-Halabia*, p. 408

28) *The Spirit of the Islamic Religion* by Afif Abd Al-Fattah, 9th Ed.

29) Sura 53, *An-Najm* (the Star) in its original form, which Muhammad later claimed came from Satan, not Gabriel. See the Qur'an translated by Rodwell (1861), Sura 53, Footnote #7.

Muhammad's mouth and heart to praise the idols of
Quraish while he was reciting the Sura of the *Najm*
(star).[30] This was the proof that Muhammad could
never distinguish between Satan and the angel, even
though it does not require much effort to realize that
praising the idols of Quraish is of the devil.

But did an angel really appear to Muhammad? Or was
that angel a making of his own imagination? I am sure that
was no angel. First, God's angel is an angel of peace and assurance. For example, when the angel came to Mary to tell
her of the birth of Christ, the first thing he said was, "Peace
be to you." She was filled with peace, faith and joy. She was
not choked, nor did she experience nervous shock or nervous breakdown, bad headache, and rolling of the eyes. Real
angels come with peace not with symptoms of epilepsy!

Second, did not "Gabriel" know the right time to visit
Muhammad, not to arrive when he was sitting in his wife's
lap? What angel could not realize this very simple matter?

Third, would an angel come down upon him with some
verses, then the next day delete them, as it happened in Sura
of *An-Najm* and others? Such verses have forced the Qur'an
interpreter to come up with something called "the nullifying
and the nullified," meaning that the better verse replaces a
verse that they believed was a mistake in the Qur'an, or one
verse would sound better than another on the same subject
– as if Muhammad's god said, "Oops!"

This chapter records Muhammad's birth, upbringing and
the coming down of the revelation upon him. I leave it to
the reader to judge whether a sound mind could accept as
reasonable what happened in the life of Muhammad.

---

30) *The Causes of Descendancy* (Asbab Al-Nuzul) by Al-Suyuti, Vol. III, p.
229.

2

Muhammad's 23 Marriages

Before I plunge deeper into this subject, the following facts should be mentioned. Muhammad said,

"I am only a human like you."[31]

The Qur'an states that Muhammad is just *a messenger*, even though Muslims consider him the supreme prophet. Yet he is considered a human who lived and died just like everyone else. In other words, the Qur'an that descended on Muhammad did *not* give him any special characteristics to distinguish him from any other human. However, it is strangely self-contradictory that the Qur'an *did* distinguish him by giving him more privileges and less obligations.

Muhammad was just a human in the Qur'an's point of view and in his own sight. Nevertheless, he enjoyed rights and privileges like no other human. He was allowed to obtain more money than others, and he granted himself more rights than them. As far as obligations are concerned, he was privileged. He was not required to comply to duties as others

---

31) See Sura *Al-Kahf* (the Cave) 18:110 and Sura *Ha Mim Sajdah* (Revelations Well-Expounded) 41:6.

were. His Muslim nation was forced to meet the obligations and expenses of the houses he opened and to keep the
people in them at a high standard of living.

For example, the Qur'an gave Muslims the right to marry
a maximum of four wives. But the Qur'an says:

> "O, Prophet, we have made lawful to thee thy wives
> to whom thou hast paid their dowers; and those
> whom thy right hand possesses out of the prisoners
> of war whom Allah has assigned to thee; and daugh-
> ters of thy parental uncles and aunts, and daugh-
> ters of thy maternal uncles and aunts, who migrated
> (from Mecca) with thee; and any believing woman
> who dedicates her soul to the prophet if the prophet
> wishes to wed her. This only for thee and not for
> the believers (at large); we know what we have ap-
> pointed for them as to their wives and the captives
> whom their right hands possess; in order that there
> should be no difficulty for thee. And Allah is Oft-
> Forgiving, Most Merciful."[32]

According to the above Qur'an verse, Allah was not satisfied just giving Muhammad many wives, so he gave him a
carte blanche to do as he wished. Allah did not even limit the
number of women he could marry, as he had with all other
Muslims. Rather, he gave him the right to grab any woman
he desired, even married ones, forcing the husband to divorce his wife when the prophet desired to marry her.

One of the greatest Muslim scholars, Burhan El-Deen
Al-Halabi, discussed the extraordinary rights and privileges
of Muhammad in his well-known book, *Al-Sira Al-Halabia*.
Al-Halabi said:

---

32) Sura *Al-Ahzab* (the Allies) 33:50.

"If Muhammad desired an unmarried woman, he has the right to enter into her (marry her) without the ceremony of marriage and without any witnesses or guardians. Not even her consent was necessary. But, if the woman was married, and Muhammad expressed his desires towards her, it becomes a must for her husband to divorce her, so that Muhammad could marry her. Also, Muhammad had the right to give that woman in marriage to any man that he chooses, without her consent. He even could get married during the season of pilgrimage, as he did with Maymouna. He also had the right to choose of the captives whomever he wanted, before the distribution of the spoils of war."[33]

"Muhammad said of himself that he was a human, and the Qur'an described him as a human. How then did he give himself more rights than all of us?"

This was said by his uncle Abu Al-Hakam in the court-yard of the Ka'aba, which was once for idol worshipers and now for the Muslims. I also ask "Was it logical or fair for a man to divorce his wife just because Muhammad desired her? Was it fair for Muhammad to buy or sell a woman, or give her in marriage to whomever he wanted, without her consent? It's far from God to accept such injustice, or to consent to such a ridiculous mockery.

Could that be the behavior of a prophet? *Another* prophet Muhammad mentions in the Qur'an stated in His Gospel:

"But I say unto you, That whosoever looketh on a woman to lust after her hath committed adultery with her already in his heart."[34]

---

33) *Al-Sira Al-Halabia*, Vol. III, p. 377.
34) Matthew 5:28

Why does Allah give Muhammad the right to lust, divorce, and marry, since he *never* gave those rights to any of the prophets? The true God would never make exceptions to His moral laws for anyone.

Remember, Muhammad gave himself the right to marry without witnesses or a marriage ceremony, or even the woman's consent. According to Islamic jurisprudence, which *he* instituted, such actions were adultery! The adulterer and the adulteress will end in "the fire of hell." [35] But Muhammad, who is a human like us according to his statement and the Qur'an's, could marry even without the required marriage ceremony that he instituted, and *without witnesses.*

When Muhammad was asked about this, he said "Gabriel" was the witness. Poor "Gabriel," wasn't he unfairly referred to, used and abused? For if "Gabriel" was considered a witness at Muhammad's weddings, where was the second witness that Islamic jurisprudence required? Why do we not see his signature on any of the marriage contracts? Where was the required guardian? Weren't those required marriage components in Islam needed when Muhammad got married? What do you think, O sons of Islam?

As Al-Halabi stated in his book, if Muhammad desired a married woman, her husband had to divorce her so the prophet could marry her. What are people thinking, to accept such teachings? Is it possible that more than one billion Muslims are confused? Where are the educated people? Don't they read their own books? It seems sure that they do not understand what they read, for I was one Muslim who did not read to understand, but rather I read for the sake of reading only – and when I did read, I did not understand.

35) See the *Hadith* of Sahih Bukhari, Vol. 2, Book 23, #468 and Vol. 9, Book 87, #171.

But now, many questions arise concerning many vital issues. How can a prophet lust after someone else's wife and demand that her husband divorce her so he can sleep with her? Where is the holy relation between a husband and his wife? Where is the institution of marriage and its protection? How could "the messenger of Allah"— and God is innocent of such a sending — do something so unholy that it would infuriate God and men? How could the prophet demand that a man marry a woman without her consent? How could a woman be coerced to marry someone without her acquiescence? Are women in Islam deprived of their humanity and/or their human rights? Are women considered animals that they should blindly obey man or "the prophet?"

The most important item in any marriage is *mutual consent*. But it seemed that what was right for Muhammad was not right for others, since he was the prophet of Allah. Because God's prophets did not act in such a manner, I have become sure that Muhammad had his own special god; for the God we worship is the God of justice, love and compassion. He is the God of Truth and not of injustice – far different from the unfair and unjust god Muhammad portrayed.

Allah granted to Muhammad extraordinary rights… and not in his legal marriages only. Muhammad had the "legal right" to *all women* – and no Muslim could object. Whenever any questions were raised, "Gabriel" came down from heaven with a verse justifying Muhammad's actions.

Before I go into the details about Muhammad's wives, it is important to mention that Muhammad was engaged to thirty women, but it was said that he was legally married to only twenty-three, and that he only knew twelve sexually. As for his many handmaids, six had offerend themselves to the prophet, but only four were preferred.[36] Ibn Kathir added that the prophet knew as wives thirteen women, and not twelve as Al-Halabi wrote.[37]

1. Khadija bint Khuwaylid

Muhammad's first wife was Khadija, the daughter of Khuwaylid. She was a well-known lady of Mecca, a rich widow who inherited her wealth from her dead husband. When she married Muhammad, she was forty years old and he was twenty-five. Here the reason for their marriage becomes obvious. Muhammad was very poor, and his uncle, Abu Talib, who became his guardian after the death of his grandfather, was poorer still. For this reason, Muhammad could not get married, even though he was five years past the normal marrying age of twenty at the oldest. Muhammad's marriage to Khadija was done by the mediation of Nawfal, the uncle of Khadija, with premarital conditions including a wedding in a church. His uncle, Abu Talib, agreed to the conditions and said: "Praises be to Allah who took away our distress and lifted up our worries."

When I attended elementary through high school, the religion teachers always said that Muhammad married many women, mainly to strengthen Islam, to enrich it with new tribal blood and to strengthen the ties between the Muslims. It was obvious to me and other students that those teachers were lying; and they spoke as though they did not know what they were talking about. They only repeated what their predecessors said. However, we learned that none of Muhammad's marriages justified our teachers' claim. On the contrary, they were all based solely on personal interest, and

---

36) See *Al-Sira Al-Halabia*, by Al-Halabi, p. 417.

37) See *The Beginning and the End (Al Bidayah wa-Nihaya)* by Ismail Ibn Kathir, Vol. 5.

only to meet *his* needs, whether for money, as with Khadija, or for beauty and sex, as with the rest of his wives.

Khadija died when she was close to seventy, while he was almost fifty-four. During their marriage, Muhammad could not marry another woman. I find it proper at the end of discussing Muhammad's marriage to Khadija to quote what Dr. Aisha Abdul Rahman (known as bint Al-Shati') said in her book, *The Wives of the Prophet*:

> "Muhammad found in Khadija the motherly compassion that he lost in his infancy."[38]

There may be much truth in that statement. Plus, remember his poverty. Muhammad begat four daughters in that first marriage.

2. Aisha bint Abu Bakr

All Muslim historians agree that Muhammad got married immediately after the death of Khadija.[39] Other Muslim historians who reported that fact also agree that Khawla the daughter of Hakim Al-Silmiyya asked Muhammad: "Will you marry a virgin or a non-virgin?" He answered: "A virgin or a non-virgin."[40] She said to him: "A virgin is Aisha and a non-virgin is Sawda bint Zam'a; take whichever you desire." He answered, "I will marry both. Tell them." She did, and Muhammad married *both* of them.[41]

These other writers made a very obvious mistake; in re-

---

38) *The Wives of the Prophet* by Dr. bint Al-Shati', p. 54.
39) See *The Life of the Prophet's Wives* by Dr. Sa'id 'Ashur, pp. 37 & 49; *Asad Al Ghaba (The Lion of the Forest)* by Ibn Al-Athir, p. 189; *Al-Isaba fi tamyiz al-Sahaba*, Part IV, p. 330; & *The Wives of the Prophet* by Al-Shati', pp. 59-60.
40) In other words, he would marry either one: a virgin *or* non-virgin.
41) For a similar story see *Muhammad: His Life Based on the Earliest Sources* by Martin Lings (1983), p. 106.

ality, Khawla did not mention Aisha, but rather she said: "the daughter of your friend Abu Bakr," meaning the older daughter Asma', not Aisha. It was more logical for her to mean eighteen-year-old Asma', because Aisha was only six. How could she have mentioned Aisha and not Asma'? *But Muhammad chose to marry six-year-old Aisha over her big sister Asma'!*

In another story about his marriage to Aisha, she came to Muhammad's house, sent by her father, carrying a plate full of dates. She entered his house while he was praying, and she stood close to him. After he finished his prayers, he touched her gown and said: "Tell your father, we have accepted what Khawla said, we have accepted, we have accepted."

Muhammad married Aisha when she was six, but he did not know her sexually until she was nine years old. Is there a moral law in this world that would allow a six-year-old girl to marry a man who is more than fifty years old? If something like this happened in a society with civil laws, such a man would be thrown in jail, or would be accused of being crazy and committed to an insane asylum. I wished that such a story was untrue, but unfortunately, all Islamic references ascertain its credibility and truth. For this I asked:

"How could I, or any other, walk behind a prophet with such a bizarre logic and outlandish behavior?"

Could it be that Allah chose a Messenger whose whole concern was to marry women and have sex with them? What kind of a god would command such marriages? How could Allah be so unjust, knowing that Muslim scholars state:

"Allah directed and guided him to those marriages?"

In other words, Muhammad was a toy in the hand of Muhammad and not in the hand of his god. He did all he wanted and attributed it to poor "Gabriel" and to Allah, who gave him whatever he desired. What a wasted life I lived and what a wasted life my Muslim kinfolk live, in the East and the West! Was it a prophet that we believed and followed? This is a question that needs a clear answer without any fanaticism. We need an answer that comes from conscience and from the Truth, not from fear and pride.

Muhammad's marriage to a child seems to have been a psychological complex resulting from his marriage to Khadija, who was fifteen years his senior. Muhammad desired to sleep with little girls, and not only with Aisha, as explained by Abbas Ibn Hisham and Ibn Hajar who said:

> "The Messenger of Allah said, when he saw Um Habib bint Abbas, while she was yet an infant: 'When she reaches the age while I am alive, I will marry her.' At that time, she was *three years old*, and he was sixty." He died two years later, wishing that she were six or nine years old, as Aisha was, so he could have married her. I am not fabricating these things against someone who was my own prophet at one time. Rather, these things were the cause of my alienation away from him and his alleged prophethood. You can read what Ibn Hajar wrote in his book,[42] as well as what Imam As-Suhaili recorded.[43]

Do not forget that those references were written by some of the greatest Muslim scholars ever.

When Muhammad died, Aisha was about eighteen years old. Young women at her age were still in their fathers' home, waiting for a husband. But that poor young widow, eighteen years old, was strictly forbidden to remarry after Muhammad. The wives of the prophet were not allowed to remarry

---

42) *Al-Isaba fi tamyiz al-Sahaba*, Vol. IV, p. 422.
43) *Rawd al-Unuf*, Vol. III, p. 66.

or to mate after Muhammad, according to Qur'anic teaching. Why did Allah do that? Where was the justice in that? And we Muslims say that one of Allah's attributes is justice? He is "most merciful and most compassionate." Then where was mercy and compassion, that he would forbid Aisha and several other wives from remarrying after Muhammad, when we were told that Muhammad was just a human like us with no superhuman abilities?

I cannot continue discussing the life of the Mother of all believers, Aisha, lest I cause her some injustice. It was enough that she suffered as a result of being a child-bride at the age of nine to a man who was older than her own father. It only added to that catastrophe that she was not allowed to remarry after his death.

3. Zainab bint Jahsh

Muhammad's third marriage is a story of great tragedy, filled with nothing but lust, sex and sensual desires. As you read, ask yourself, "Where were the tribal ties in this story?" "What did this marriage have to do with Muhammad's supposed calling?"

The story began when Zayd Ibn Haritha was kidnapped from his aristocratic family by some traveling Arabians who sold him to Khadija, the first wife of Muhammad, who in turn gave him as a present to her husband, Muhammad, to be his servant. But after Muhammad heard his calling to Islam, he freed Zayd and he adopted him for a son publicly, where he said, "Zayd is my son, I inherit him and he inherits me." Thereafter, he was called "Zayd, the son of Muhammad."

Later, he asked Zainab, his cousin on his father's side, to marry Zayd. She first refused because Zayd was homely. Furthermore, even though Muhammad adopted him publicly,

he was considered by the majority of the Arabs as a slave.
For this reason, she could not bring herself to love him, so
she said to Muhammad, "If you insist on me marrying him,
I will, but I'd rather marry you, not Zayd." Muhammad insisted that she marry Zayd, and so it was. To convince her
to marry Zayd, a verse had to descend upon Muhammad
from heaven that commanded Zainab and all the Muslims
to obey him:

> "It is not fitting for a believer, man or woman, when
> a matter has been decided by Allah and his Messen-
> ger, to have any option about their decision; if any-
> one disobeys Allah and his Messenger, he is indeed
> on a clearly wrong path."[44]

Thus, Zainab married Zayd. Up to this point, the matter
could seem logical despite all of the coercion and duress that
were imposed upon Zainab. But what happened thereafter
was very peculiar, shocking and appalling.

The story goes on to tell us that one day Muhammad went
to visit his adopted son Zayd. When he entered the house,
Zayd was not home. Muhammad saw Zainab half naked
as she was putting her clothes on. Muhammad desired her,
but he was afraid to enter the house and commit adultery
with her. As he was leaving, he said to her, "Praise be to Allah who changes hearts." Zainab smiled and later told Zayd
about that visit and Muhammad's statement. Zayd went immediately to Muhammad and asked him: "Do you want me
to divorce her for you?" Muhammad answered him: "Hold
unto your wife and fear Allah." That was initially a noble
stand on the part of Muhammad. However, what filled
Muhammad's heart and soul was totally different than what
his lips expressed, for he really desired her as was reported

---

44) Sura *Al-Ahzab* (the Allies) 33:36 (Yusuf Ali).

by Al-Zamkhashri: "The external appearance of Muham-mad differed from what was inside him."[45] Simply put, on the outside it appeared that Muhammad did not want Zayd to divorce Zainab. But his intentions were the opposite: for Muhammad fell in love with Zainab when he saw her half naked.[46]

The Qur'an tells us that when Muhammad saw Zainab half naked, he fell in love with her, and wanted her as his wife. However, he hesitated because of what people would say about him, snatching the wife of his adopted son. But Muhammad's god came to reprimand him for his hesita-tion. Strangely, it was Allah who wanted the woman to leave her husband, and to violate all moral laws, so Muhammad could have her. And it's in plain sight in the Qur'an:

> "Behold, thou didst say to whom who had received the grace of Allah and thy favour, 'Retain thou (in wedlock) thy wife, and fear Allah.' But thou didst hide in thy heart that which Allah was about to make manifest: thou didst fear the people, but it is more fitting that thou shouldst fear Allah. Then when Zayd had dissolved (his marriage) with her, with the necessary (formality), we joined her in marriage to thee."[47]

Little time passed between Sura 33:36, where Allah en-couraged Zayd to stay married, and 33:37, where the god of Muhammad commanded Zayd to leave Zainab so Muham-mad could marry her. What caused that god to change his mind? Was that god a toy in Muhammad's hand, so a new verse would come down to annul the verse that came before

---

45) *Al-Kashaf* by Al-Zamkhashri, Vol. III, p. 54.

46) *The Wives of the Prophet* by bint Al-Shati', pp. 158 & 164.

47) Sura *Al-Ahzab* (the Allies) 33:37.

(the one that encouraged Zayd to keep his wife)? Did not Allah *command* Zayd to stay married to Zainab? Was his god unable to keep their house together? How could Muhammad's god find it easy to destroy a home, so Muhammad's desires could be met? Was that a god of justice and mercy?

In his book, *The Life of Muhammad*, Dr. Haikal objected to this story about Zayd and Zainab. He described it as shameful, and he accused missionaries and western researchers of fabricating it, trying to demean Islam and its prophet. When I was a Muslim, I wished that Dr. Haikal was right, and that all those defamation stories against Muhammad were just make-believe fabrications.

However, let us confront the bitter fact, and read the reply of Dr. bint Al-Shati', a renowned, well-read Muslim scholar, who stated the naked truth:

> "The story of Muhammad, the Messenger, admiring Zainab ... and the story of Muhammad leaving her house saying, Praise Allah who changes the hearts, were told to us by good predecessors such as Imam Al-Tabari in his history book, and by Abu Ja'far Ibn Habib Al-Nabeh, and the beloved Al-Tabari, and the neighbor of Allah, Al-Zamkhashri. Those people told us the story before the world heard of the Crusades, evangelization and western missionaries. It is a right thing to leave their notion aside, and let us look at this case as it was told by the two Tabaris and by Ibn Habib. Why should we deny that the Messenger was a human who looked at someone like Zainab and admired her? Muhammad had never claimed that his heart was in his hand turning it whichever direction he wanted, neither did he ever allege that he was infallible, without human lust. As

he got excited seeing Aisha (more by Aisha than the other wives), he said, 'Allah, do not blame me for not possessing what you possess (self-control).'"[48]

Al-Zamkhashri, a great Muslim Imam, said:

"The Messenger of Allah saw Zainab, after he gave her in marriage to Zayd, and he fell in love with her, and said, Praise Allah, who changes things."

Forget the missionaries and the western evangelists. Just look at the source of the Islamic story according to the imams of the early centuries of Islam. What was said above by bint Al-Shati', an accomplished Muslim historian, will clear any and all doubts.

First, the greatest Muslim scholars verified and affirmed that the story of Zayd and Zainab was true.

Second, Muhammad was not immune from lust and erotic passion. He was a human with a human heart that loved and hated, accepted something one day, and rejecting it the next. And Allah supported Muhammad in all his decisions no matter what they were.

Moreover, Allah's endorsement of Muhammad's actions was recorded in the two Qur'an verses mentioned above, where he commanded Zayd to marry Zainab in one, and later, he sent down a verse commanding the same man to divorce his wife so Muhammad could marry her. How could Almighty God, the Just God, agree to such an atrocity? How could the Messenger of Allah lust after someone else's wife, and how could he lust after his adopted son's wife? Isn't lusting and acting on the lust after another man's wife a crime?

Should we say, "Praise be to Allah who made lawful to Muhammad what he makes unlawful to the rest of the world?"

---

48) *The Wives of the Prophet* by bint Al-Shati', pp.61 & 63.

Remember, Muhammad claimed to be a human like us, without infallibility and without any special privileges. Are each one of us supposed to have our own god and our own "Gabriel" so we can do what we want and reject what we don't desire, alleging that god commanded, and that "Gabriel" brought down the verse that justified us?

It would be possible to overlook such acts if done by an ordinary or unbelieving man. But how can we overlook them when they were done by someone who claimed to be a prophet of Allah such as Muhammad, who is supposed to be the example of our life and our behavior?

Let us compare this to the life of King David, "the prophet David" to Muslims. David lusted after the wife of another man. But though he was much beloved of God, God did not let the affair slide by just because David was a prophet and a king. Rather, God severely reprimanded and punished him. God's threat rang throughout Israel, as He said to David:

> "Now, therefore, the sword shall never depart from thine house because thou hast despised me and hast taken the wife of Uriah the Hittite to be thy wife."[49]

Consequently, David repented with tears:

> "Have mercy upon me, O God, according to thy lovingkindness… Wash me thoroughly from mine iniquity, and cleanse me from my sin. For I acknowledge my transgressions: and my sin is ever before me… Create in me a clean heart, O God, and renew a right spirit within me"[50]

In other words, God is a holy, pure God who does not compromise His holiness for any person's sins, whether it

---

49) 2 Samuel 12:9
50) Psalm 51:1-3, 10

is David's or Muhammad's. The True God punishes sin. He
does not reward it, ever! Consequently, the sword wreaked
havoc in David's family.

Likewise, Muhammad behaved the same. Could that be
the reason the sword has been wreaking havoc in his nation
ever since it started? Since the inception of Islam, killing,
murdering, and oppression have been the norm.

Nevertheless, let's get back to the story of Zainab. Muhammad did not wait, as was traditional in such situations.
(Such a transitional period is required by Islam, but was not
applicable to Muhammad.) Zainab herself explained:

> "After the divorce, immediately, and behold, the
> prophet of Allah entered my house while I was
> without a head-cover, and I asked him, 'Is it going
> to be like this without a guardian or a witness?' He
> answered me, 'Allah is the guardian and "Gabriel"
> is the witness.'" As a result of his statement, Zainab
> boasted in front of Muhammad's other wives, say-
> ing: "Your fathers gave you in marriage, but as for
> me, it was heaven who gave me in marriage, to the
> Messenger of Allah."[51]

During his lifetime, Arabs and Muslims criticized Muhammad's behavior, saying he married the divorcée of his
own son, which was not legal. But for Muhammad to get
out of such a predicament, "Gabriel" was ready to bring
down a verse from his god, stating he had never adopted
Zayd. Therefore, marrying Zainab would be legal:

> "Muhammad is not the father of any of your men,
> but he is the Messenger of Allah, and the seal of

---

51) For more information, read *The Jurisprudence of the Life of Muhammad*
(Faqh Al-Sirah) by Sa'id 'Ashur, p. 126; and *Al-Isaba fi tamyiz al-Sahaba*
by Ibn Hajar Asqaliani, Vol. IV, p. 307.

the prophets: and Allah has full knowledge of all things."[52]

This verse made it seem as though Muhammad had forgotten that he told the Muslims a short time before, "Zayd is my son, I inherit him and he inherits me." And it is obvious that he did not care that his actions were the cause of abolishing adoption in Islam (even to this day), just because of his lustful relation with Zainab. In other words, people from around the world adopt Muslim orphans to alleviate their misery, but a Muslim family would not adopt a Muslim orphan, to keep from repeating the story of Zayd and Zainab in their families.

It seems that everyone and everything had to work together to satisfy the lust of Muhammad, including all the Muslims and the archangel "Gabriel." Everyone was supposed to be prepared to do all things necessary, even give up one's wife, and violate all moral laws, so Muhammad could be happy. What a prophet! What an example!

I should end the story of Muhammad's marriage to Zainab bint Jahsh with a statement made by a great Muslim scholar and recorded in his book, *Al-Sira Al-Halabia*:

"If Muhammad lusted after a married woman, it became a must for her husband to divorce her for him."[53]

Al-Suyuti said:

"Muhammad entered into Zainab without permission."[54]

What mature mind can accept such an immoral incursion,

---

52) Sura *Al-Ahzab* (the Allies) 33:40.

53) *Al-Sira Al-Halabia* by Al-Halabi, Vol. III, p. 377.

54) *The Causes of Descendancy* (Asbab Al-Nuzul) by Al-Suyuti, p. 221.

let alone boast about it? Could that really be the behavior of "the prophet of God?" Was it really "in the interest of Islam and the Muslims," for Muhammad to marry Zainab?

4. Safiya bint Huyay

Muhammad's fourth marriage was to Safiya, the daughter of Huyay, the Jew. It was in the seventh year of Hijra,[55] when Muhammad gave the order to raid the tribe of Khaybar. During that raid, many of Khaybar's men were killed and many possessions were looted and their women were taken captive. Those taken captive included Safiya, her husband, Kinana, son of Rabi'a, and her father. Muhammad ordered her father killed, and her husband tortured until he divulged the hiding place of his money. After he told them, Muhammad ordered him killed, then married his wife (talk about romance). Could there be more cruelty than that?

After the raid, Dihya Al-Kalbi, one of Muhammad's close companions (Muhammad said that "Gabriel," the archangel, had the same beautiful countenance as his[56]), asked Muhammad for some of the captive women. Muhammad said: "Go and take whichever suits you." Dihya took Safiya, but his joy did not last long because one of the men said to Muhammad: "Oh prophet of Allah, have you given Safiya to Dihya? For you are the only one that deserves to have her." Muhammad said: "Bring here Dihya and Safiya."

When they came to his presence and he saw beautiful Safiya, he said to Dihya, "Go and take another woman." Then he ordered his personal chamber lady to prepare Safi-

---

55) The Hijra is the year Muhammad emigrated to Medina, or 622 AD. The Battle of Khaybar took place in May of 629 AD.
56) See the *Hadith* of Sahih Bukhari, Vol. 4, Book 56, #827; Vol. 6, Book 61, #503; and the *Hadith* of Sahih Muslim, Book 1, #321 & Book 31, #6006.

ya, so he could enter into her that same night. Umm Salma described Safiya:

> "I have never seen in all my life a more beautiful woman than Safiya. Women used to travel a distance just to take a look at Safiya and her beauty."[57]

When Muhammad entered into Safiya, she was only seventeen years old, in her first month of marriage to Kinana, whom Muhammad had ordered to be killed. At that time Muhammad was sixty-two years old. Three years later she became a widow for the second time, when Muhammad died. But this time she was not allowed to remarry. Where was the justice, that by the order of Muhammad and the god of Muhammad, those wives were not allowed to remarry? Did that come from God? I think not.

We always believed that the prophet married those ladies to strengthen the ties of Islam or because he wanted to have mercy on them. But now my sight is clearer and my understanding better as I look at his marriages to Khadija, Aisha, Zainab, and Safiya.

5. Juwayriyyah bint Al-Harith

The fifth marriage was to poor Juwayriyyah bint Al-Harith. Juwayriyyah was twenty years old when Muhammad, at fifty-nine, married her. (Muhammad married Juwayriyyah one year *before* he married Safiya.) I will let Muhammad's first victim, Aisha, who is known as the Mother of the Believers, tell the story:

---

57) See the *Hadith* of Sahih Bukhari, Vol. 1, Book 8, #367; Vol. 2, Book 14, #68; Vol. 3, Book 34, #431; and the *Hadith* of Sahih Muslim, Book 8, #3325, 3328 & 3329. See also *The Life of the Prophet by Ibn Hisham, p. 179; Al-Sira Al-Halabia by Al-Halabi, Vol. III, p. 145; and The Wives of the Prophet by bint Al-Shati', pp. 182-185. More on Sa ya is in Chapter 4 of this book.*

"When Allah's Messenger distributed the captives of the children of Mustaliq, Juwayriyyah was given to Thabit bin Qais.[58] She was a woman in her twenties and exceedingly beautiful. No one saw her without strongly admiring her. When I saw her at the door of my house, I hated her, because I was sure that the Messenger of Allah would see in her what I saw of her beauty."[59]

Muhammad did choose the most beautiful and the youngest women to marry. Aisha was nine, Zainab was twenty, Safiya was seventeen, and Juwayriyyah was twenty, when he himself was between fifty-five and sixty years old.

Where were the ties among Muslims in any of these marriages, and especially his marriage to a Jew? Was it compassion for her that he married her, after he bribed Thabit with money to leave her alone? This is a question I ask Muslims.

6. Umm Salma

The sixth marriage of Muhammad was to another beautiful lady named Umm Salma. Aisha, the first of Muhammad's victims, said:

"When Allah's Messenger married Umm Salma, I was stricken with great sadness as he spoke of her beauty, but when I saw her, I saw [many-fold] what he described."[60]

---

58) A trusted friend of Muhammad, known as "the orator of Allah's Apostle." See the *Hadith* of Sahih Bukhari, Vol. 5, Book 59, #659 & 662; and the *Hadith* of Sahih Muslim, Book 1, #215 & Book 29, #5650.
59) See *The Life of the Prophet* (Sirat Al-Nabi) by Ibn Ishaq & *The Wives of the Prophet* by bint Al-Shati', pp. 173-176, "The Beautiful Captive." This is found in another form in *Sunan Abu-Dawud*, Book 29, #3920 and *Muhammad: His Life Based on the Earliest Sources* by Martin Lings (1983), pp. 241-242.
60) *The Wives of the Prophet*, p. 137.

Umm Salma was the daughter of 'Uthman (his third successor), bin Affan's sister. When Muhammad first saw her at 'Uthman's house, he asked about her, and 'Uthman answered, "She is my niece, and her husband is…" Twenty-four hours later, Muhammad ordered her husband, Ghassan bin Mughira, to carry the flag at the front in the coming battle. He did, and he died in that battle. The next day, Muhammad entered into Umm Salma. That is how she became his wife.

Strange is the life of this prophet. Could he not be satisfied with women? What was his real opinion of women? Was a woman just a bondmaid under his feet? Was she only a bond-slave to be ready to jump in bed at his whim and prepare his food and drink? Did he not think of the feelings of Aisha, whom he called near-stationed to him, as he added new women to his list of wives? Did he not think of Safiya who lost her husband, but whom he married immediately as though her loss meant nothing?

What god was that who had no job other than making sure that Muhammad's sex life was satisfied? What god would make sure that a husband was killed, or a woman divorced so Muhammad could have a woman he desired? My Righteous God is above those iniquities, and woe unto them when they stand before the Real God on the Day of Judgment. Do we wonder why violence is ripping through Islamic circles?

7. Sawda bint Zam'a

This is the story of Muhammad's marriage to Sawda bint Zam'a. She was the only homely woman among the wives of Muhammad. However, most Muslim historians describe her as good-hearted and very beautiful on the inside.

When Khadija died, Khawla bint Hakim came to Muhammad, and she asked him, "Do you want a virgin or a

non-virgin?" He asked her to bring him both. She told him
that the virgin was Bakr's daughter and the non-virgin was
Sawda; and he chose both. But he was surprised to discover,
on his wedding night that Sawda was not beautiful. Muhammad was angry, and he reprimanded Khawla for intro-
ducing Sawda to him. Ibn Hajar Asqalani wrote:

> "Khawla, in redeeming her action, she offered her-
> self to him (to Muhammad), and he lived with her
> as husband and wife, and that was only two months
> after his marriage to Sawda."[61]

Dr. bint Al-Shati' said in her book:

> "When the night of Sawda came (where he spent
> the night with her), Muhammad told her of his de-
> cision to divorce her. She heard the news with great
> surprise, and she felt as though the walls were fall-
> ing down on her. So she begged him, 'Please, keep
> me, O Messenger of Allah.' He answered her, 'On
> one condition, that you give your appointed night to
> Aisha.' Instead of spending those appointed nights
> with Sawda, he would spend them with Aisha along
> with the nights that are already appointed for her.
> Sawda agreed, saying, 'From now on, I will not want
> what women want, for I give my appointed night to
> Aisha.' As a result, Muhammad kept her as a wife,
> but he never visited her."[62]

That was the only wife among Muhammad's women who
was not physically beautiful. However, Muhammad's wife
acknowledged she was the most beautiful in character and
morals. But as far as Muhammad was concerned, character,
morals and the beauty of the soul were of no importance.

61) *Al-Isaba fi tamyiz al-Sahaba* by Ibn Hajar, Vol. IV, p. 284
62) *The Wives of the Prophet* by bint Al-Shati', pp. 66-67

For this reason he threatened to divorce her if she did not agree to give her night to Aisha. How could that be decent behavior, O Messenger of Allah?

8. Umm Habiba (Ramlah) bint Abu-Sufyan

Umm Habiba was first married to Ubayd-Allah bin Jahsh who was the son of Muhammad's aunt, and the brother of Zainab that he married a week earlier. What happened and how did that wedding take place? Ubayd-Allah confronted Muhammad and said to him: "You are not a prophet nor a messenger of Allah. Stop claiming that. I am a believer in Christ for He is the Truth, but you are a self-conceited man." Ubayd was forced to leave, and Muhammad married his wife, Umm Habiba, to plant sorrow and sadness in his heart. At that time, Umm Habiba was a beautiful woman, twenty-three years old.[63]

9. Maryam Qibtiyyah (Maria the Egyptian)

Muhammad's story with Maria the Egyptian had a different turn. Amro bin Al-Aaz carried a letter from Muhammad to Al-Muqawqis, the ruler of Egypt, calling him to embrace Islam. Knowing Muhammad's weakness, and in order to gain his favor, he gave Muhammad as a present two very beautiful sisters. Had it not been for the earlier coming down of a Qur'anic verse that forbade the marrying of two sisters, Muhammad would have done it. Even so, he almost violated his own laws and married them both, except for his father-in-law Umar's advice, warning him against such action. It was reported that Muhammad loved Maria and used to visit her often and spent many hours both day and night with her without getting bored.[64]

---

63) See *The Wives of the Prophet* by bint Al-Shati', p. 203.
64) See *Al-Isaba fi tamyiz al-Sahaba* by Ibn Hajar Asqalani, Part VII, p. 291 and *The Wives of the Prophet*, p. 217.

The story says that Maria wanted to meet Muhammad, so she went to see him at the house of his wife Hafsa, the daughter of Umar, who was not home at that time. But when Hafsa suddenly returned home, she found Muhammad having intercourse with Maria in her own bed! She said to Muhammad:

> "In my own house, and in my own bed, and on [my] appointed day..." The prophet, upon whom Allah's revelation came down, said: "Keep that secret, and do not tell anyone. Do not tell Aisha," (for he trembled with fear of Aisha). He continued: "I will never touch Maria again. And I declare to you that your father and Aisha's father will rule over my nation after me. I have bequeathed that to them." But Hafsa told Aisha, and Muhammad divorced Hafsa.[65]

When news of the divorce reached her father, Umar, he became very angry, and almost left Islam. When Muhammad heard about Umar's reaction, he took Hafsa back, by a command from poor "Gabriel," who told him:

> "Hafsa will be your wife on the resurrection day."[66]

Muhammad decided to abandon Maria in order to satisfy Hafsa and Umar. However, the problem of self-deprivation and desertion of Maria remained. How could Muhammad solve all those problems? As usual, Qur'anic verses from Muhammad's god, who made available those saving verses to Muhammad, were there for him. In this case, the Sura *Al-Tahrim* (of the Deprivation) came down to reprimand Muhammad for depriving Maria of his affections, for Allah had mercy on His Messenger because of the hardship he

---

65) See the *Sunan Abu-Dawud*, Book 12, #2276.
66) See the *Hadith* of Sahih Bukhari, Vol. 3, Book 43, #648 and Sura *Al-Ahzab* (the Allies) 33:28-29.

imposed upon himself (depriving himself of Maria). Let us read this Sura, which allowed Muhammad to restore relations with Maria and annulled the deprivation:

"O Prophet, why holdest thou to be forbidden that which Allah has made lawful to thee? Thou seekest to please thy consorts. But Allah is Oft-forgiving, Most Merciful."[67]

In 66:4-5, Muhammad's god addressed the wives of Muhammad:

"If ye two [meaning Aisha and Hafsa] turn in repentance to him, your hearts are indeed so inclined; but if ye back up each other against him [meaning Muhammad], truly Allah is his protector, and Gabriel and (every) righteous one among those who believe, and furthermore, the angels will back him up. It may be, if he [Muhammad] divorced you all that Allah will give him [Muhammad] in exchange consorts better than you." Could Muhammad have a more helpful god?[68]

Before I end the story of Maria, the Egyptian, and the jealousy of Aisha and Hafsa of her, and their mutiny against Muhammad, I would like to make clear that the god of Muhammad, "Gabriel" and the companions of Muhammad were all against Aisha and Hafsa, to the extent that the god of Muhammad had to send a harsh warning to both rebellious wives, saying: "If you do not refrain from causing

---

67) Sura *Al-Tahrim* (the Deprivation), 66:1.
68) More than 20 Muslim scholars record this story, including: *Al-Istiab*, Vol. IV, p. 1812; *Oyun Al-Ithr*, Vol. II, p. 402; *Al-Samt Al-Thamin*, p. 85; *Al-Zamkhashri*, pp. 562-63; *The Causes of Descendancy* by Al-Suyuti, p. 280; *Al-Ittiqan* by Al-Suyuti, Vol. IV, p. 92; *Fuqaha' Al-Sahaba* by Abd Al-Aziz Al-Shanwi, p. 38; and *The Life of Muhammad* by Dr. Haikal, p. 450, entitled, "The Revolution of the Wives of Muhammad."

troubles to Muhammad, I, his god, will make him divorce you to marry wives better than you."

Did the Creator of this universe really have nothing better to do than solve their trivial jealousy problems of Muhammad's wives? I believe such a god is a catch, and Muhammad could not have a better god.

There is something I cannot get over. The life of Muhammad is strange, but stranger yet is to see Muslims read and see the reality of the life of Muhammad, yet they still walk behind that man. Why? In the introduction I spoke of "fear from the fearful" that rules in the Islamic world. In reality, most Muslims have knowledge of the truth about Muhammad and Islam; but intimidation, terror and fear dominate them. Death is the penalty to the apostate.[69] History tells us that Abu Bakr ordered ten thousand people killed in three days because they decided to leave Islam.

10. Maymuna bint Al-Harith

Maymuna concludes this chapter dealing with such a hurtful subject (the abuse of women), that I feel obligated to apologize on behalf of the prophet of the Muslims to all the women of the world. It is regrettable that Muhammad considered women as bondmaids and commodities to buy and sell, as though they were without feelings or rights. I tell you the story of Maymuna to clarify an important point: Muhammad prohibited many things to all others, but he permitted them to himself. Muslims know that weddings during the month of the pilgrimage (Al-Hajj[70]) are forbidden in the Qur'an.[71] Despite this fact, Muhammad married Maymuna bint Al-Harith during the pilgrimage season.

---

69) See, for example, Sura *An-Nisa'* (the Women) 4:89.
70) The last month of the Muslim lunar calendar, 3 months after Ramadan.
71) See Sura *Al-Baqara* (the Cow) 2:197.

The story begins with Maymuna telling one of her friends that she wanted to marry the prophet during the pilgrimage season. Her friend told her that she could not do that because there were clear instructions in the Qur'an prohibiting weddings during the pilgrimage season. However, Maymuna was not going to let that stop her.

Maymuna was on her camel, but when she saw Muhammad, she threw herself before him and told him that the camel and all that was on it were his. Muhammad reminded her that they were in the pilgrimage season, but Maymuna responded that she did not want to wait.

Was it possible for Muhammad to restrain himself until the end of the pilgrimage season? Past experience proved two things: he could not resist women's beauty, and the needed solution was always ready for him. That very evening, he said to her, "A verse descended onto me:

> "...And any believing woman who dedicates her soul to the prophet if the Prophet wishes to wed her – this only for thee, and not for the Believers (at large)... in order that there should be no difficulty for thee..."[72]

So Al-Abbas, Muhammad's uncle, officiated, after he commented that Muhammad was in the Hajj garment.[73] Ibn Hisham said:

> "Ibn Ishaq said that the Messenger of Allah married Maymuna during his journey (pilgrimage), and that is illegal, and the one that officiated was Abbas Ibn Abd Al-Muttalib."[74]

---

72) Sura *Al-Ahzab* (the Allies) 33:50.
73) See the *Hadith* of Sahih Bukhari, Vol. 3, Book 29, #63; Vol. 5, Book 59, #559; & the *Hadith* of Sahih Muslim, Book 8, #3283-84.
74) *The Life of the Prophet* by Ibn Hisham, Vol. III, p. 202

In this statement, Al-Bukhari and Ibn Hisham showed the contradictions that kept showing up in the life of Muhammad throughout his life.

Despite the fact that Muhammad had eleven wives, the Messenger of Allah would not wait for his wives' menstrual period to end. He entered into his wives while they were menstruating, despite the fact that it is forbidden in the Sura of The Cow.[75] In the *Hadith* of Sahih Muslim, Vol. I, page 590, Muslim says, quoting Nawawi, that Aisha said:

> "If anyone of us was having her menstrual period, Allah's Messenger ordered her to come to him for sexual intercourse while she is on the peak of her period."

Maymuna said:

> "The Messenger of Allah used to have sexual intercourse with me during my menstrual period, while a piece of garment is between us."

Umm Salma said the same thing.[76]

Muhammad got married during the pilgrimage journey when his god clearly forbade such action. He had sexual intercourse with his wives while they were having their menstrual periods, which his god also prohibited. Ask yourself: Why did Muhammad commit all those blatant violations? Surely, in the depth of his soul, he did not believe that the *real* Gabriel came to him, or that his revelation descended upon him, or that God sent down any thing upon him. How could he do all those disgusting things without reluctance? Were those the actions of a normal person? Certainly not. Then his atrocious claim that he was the prophet and Mes-

---

75) See Sura *Al-Baqara* (the Cow) 2:222.
76) See the *Hadith* of Sahih Muslim, Book 3, #577-581.

senger of Allah! It becomes certain that any *true* God would be totally innocent of such ridiculous claims.

Clearly, his life, actions and behavior never complied with God's real and holy teachings. Oh that Muslims of the earth may use their reasoning power!

3

The Dictator, The King of Racism

In this chapter you will see how Muhammad behaved in society at large. Then we will consider whether or not those actions would befit a prophet sent by God.

The Story of Ali

Ali bin Abu Talib was Muhammad's cousin and one of the ten companions who carried his message. Once he saved Muhammad's life by taking his place in bed (where he himself was almost killed) as Muhammad fled the town.[77]

Ali a well-learned young men in Mecca, who received his knowledge from his uncle, Abu Al-Hakam, himself a learned man with the largest library in Arabia. However, Muhammad and the Muslims accused him of being ignorant. A Qur'anic verse even came down from Allah, giving Abu Al-Hakam the demeaning title, *Abu-Jahl*, "the father of ignorance."[78]

---

77) For one version of these events, see *Muhammad: His Life Based on the Earliest Sources* by Martin Lings (1983), p. 117.
78) See *Muhammad: His Life Based on the Earliest Sources*, p. 58. Abu-Jahl ('Amr bin Hisham) is mentioned throughout the *Ahadith* of Sahih Bukhari and Sahi Muslim, as well as in the *Sunan Abu-Dawud*.

At the end, Ali bin Abu Talib separated himself from Muhammad, in an exciting story that we have no place for at this time. However, the most important point to understand here is the fact that a large percentage of Muslims, the Shi'ite Muslims, acknowledge that Ali was always more qualified to be the prophet than Muhammad.

The following story[79] reveals the spirit of discrimination that dominated Muhammad and his egotism, that is, what he desired for himself but did not wish others to have.

The worst thing that Fatima, Muhammad's daughter, feared was that her husband, Ali, would marry other women while she was still alive. Ali, seeing that Muhammad and the other companions each had many wives, wanted to follow in their path of marrying at least four wives, which was made legal by the Qur'an, Muhammad, "Gabriel" and Allah.

Therefore, what is legal and legitimate applying to all women, should apply to the daughters of the prophet: that is, a man can remarry up to four wives. Fatima, the daughter of Muhammad, had seen her father marry many women, as Aisha, Hafsa, Umm Salma and others. Muhammad remarried while his wives were still young and alive. The following story tells us that what is applicable to all women was not applicable to Muhammad's daughters.

When Ali announced his engagement to the daughter of 'Amr bin Hisham[80], Fatima, his wife, Muhammad's daughter was furious; and she carried her tantrum to her father. Ali's decision to remarry put Muhammad in a very disconcert-

---

79) See the *Hadith* of Sahih Bukhari, Vol. 7, Book 62, #157; *The Daughters of the Prophet* by bint Al-Shati', p. 189; *Zad Al-Ma'ad* by Ibn Qayyim Al-Jawziyya, Vol. V, p. 117; and *Rawd Al-Unuf* by Imam As-Suhaili, Vol. 4.
80) That is, the daughter of Abu Jahl (Abu Al-Hakam)

ing and embarrassing situation. Would Muhammad stand
up and support Islamic teachings that promote having many
wives, or succumb to the angry tantrum of his daughter?

Muhammad's decision was to forget his god's teachings and the instructions of "Gabriel," and succumb to his
daughter's wishes, prohibiting Ali from having wives beside
Fatima. His fatherhood and compassion forced him to forbid Ali from adding wives and having a harem like Muhammad and the rest of his companions. Muhammad did
not wish to place his most beloved daughter in a "shooting
battle" with other wives. He considered having another wife
in his daughter's husband's life as a harsh experience that his
daughter should not endure. He went to the Mosque that
week and from the pulpit, he shouted:

> "I do not permit, I do not permit, I do not permit
> him to divorce my daughter, because my daughter is
> a part of me. What hurts her, hurts me."[81]

Amazing. Why did Muhammad say that Fatima would
not have what all the other women had, regardless of their
consent – other competitors? Aisha, Hafsa, Umm Salma,
Maria, Zainab and others had to endure other wives in the
life of their husband. Why should Fatima be exempt? Did
his daughter have feelings that his own wives did not have?
Why did he accept that the beloved Aisha and his other
wives go through that harsh experience, but not his daughter? Where was the justice of the "Master of all prophets?"

I bet that if Ali insisted on his stand to remarry, a verse

---

81) Variations on this last sentence are found in the *Hadith* of Sahih
Bukhari, Vol. 5, Book 57, #61 & 111 and the *Hadith* of Sahih Muslim,
Book 31, #6000. The whole story is found in the *Hadith* of Sahih
Bukhari, Vol. 4, Book 53, #342; Vol. 5, Book 57, #76 and the *Hadith* of
Sahih Muslim, Book 31, #5999, 6001 & 6002.

from Muhammad's god would have descended the next day to prohibit Ali from marrying another wife. Don't forget that "Gabriel" was always standing by, and Muhammad's god Allah had the perfect verse for every occasion.

Muhammad argued: "Fatima is a part of me, and what hurts her, hurts me." Amazing! Was not Aisha *a part of* Abu Bakr, Muhammad's companion and his first successor? Was not Hafsa the daughter of Umar *a part of* Umar, Muhammad's companion and his second successor? It is amazing to hear how Muslims try to justify Muhammad's discriminatory decision by saying:

> "The fiancé of Ali was a Muslim, but her father was a disbeliever. For this reason, he was not allowed to marry her."

Was not Umm Salma a Muslim when Muhammad married her, and her father a disbeliever? How about Maria the Egyptian? Why was it legitimate for these daughters to marry Muhammad, but not when his own daughter was involved? Only a small minority of Muslim scholars even try to defend Muhammad with that ridiculous argument.

Having Sex with Married Women

Here is another story that can cause a person to be revolted and appalled. The Prophet of Islam said:

> "The married women among the captives are lawful for you to marry, Oh Muslims."

Some Muslims and warriors refused to accept Muhammad's declaration. After the raid of Awtas, many women were taken captive, while their husbands were still alive. Some of the Muslim warriors refused to have intercourse with those women despite the fact that Muhammad had called them to do so.

Muhammad, son of Abd Allah, the revelation receiver, declared that having intercourse with captive women was lawful. In order to convince his men, Muhammad's god was ready with a verse, and "Gabriel" was set to bring it down. Whenever his men objected, a new verse came down:

> "Also (prohibited to you are) women already married, **except those whom your right hands possess**: thus hath Allah ordained (prohibitions) against you: Except for these, all others are lawful, provided ye seek (them in marriage) with gifts from your property — desiring chastity, not lust. Seeing that ye derive benefit from them, give them their dowers (at least) as prescribed; but if, after a dower is prescribed, ye agree Mutually (to vary it), there is no blame on you, and Allah is All-knowing All-wise."[82]

It is astounding! Many Muslim scholars corroborated the story of Muhammad, making it lawful for Muslim to have intercourse with the married wives of captives.[83] Ibn Kathir mentioned the whole story:

> "Abu Sa'id Al-Khudri said, We captured some women of the captivity of Awtas, and they had their husbands. So we thought it was an iniquity to have intercourse with them. However, the Prophet commanded us to do it, but we refused. Consequently, a verse came down making their vaginas lawful to us."[84]

The real God would never command something so immoral? Was not that deliberate adultery? Worse yet, was not

---

82) Sura *An-Nisa'* (the Women) 4:24.
83) This story is confirmed in *The Causes of Descendancy* by Al-Suyuti, p. 73; in *Al-Zamkhashri*, Vol. I, p. 131; in *The Sahih* by Musnid, p. 47 and in most Islamic references.
84) *The Beginning and the End* by Ibn Kathir, Vol. IV, p. 339.

that shameful rape? Who is Muhammad's god Allah? Do Muslims have a special god that makes adultery and rape lawful? Even though we are living in the space age, much more advanced than the Bedouin age of Muhammad, adultery and rape are still accepted in Islamic countries. It is law, allowing the conqueror the right to take the captive woman, even if her husband is still alive, as Allah's gift for himself.

Would the real God legislate anything like that? Absolutely not! The God I know is a holy God, above sin, iniquity and impurity. Rather, such are the deeds of pirates, gangsters, and hard-hearted robbers who have no consideration for captive women or their wishes, because they do not believe they have any value, other than being a sex object. What law, earthly or heavenly, would allow such an atrocity?

The following statement was made by Muhammad in the Traditions, *Al-Hadith*, which in essence is the statement of a terrorist to the furthest extent:

> "He who kills someone, has the right to all his belongings."[85]

Muhammad made this statement to encourage Muslims to raid and kill. Such behavior became an enforceable law in Islamic countries, and is so even to this day. If a man kills another in a raid, instead of being tried and imprisoned for the atrocity, he has the right to take, by force, the wife of the man he killed, as well as his daughters, and all of his possessions.

Nothing can match such a sinister atrocity, which can be

---

85) See the *Hadith* of Sahih Bukhari, Vol. 4, Book 53, #370; as well as the *Hadith* of Sahih Muslim, Book 19, Chapter 13 "Regarding the Right of the Fighter to the Belongings of One Killed by Him in the Fight," #4340-4344. See also *Jawami' Al-Sira* by Ibn Hazm, p. 191 and *The Jurisprudence of the Life of Muhammad* (Faqh Al-Sira) by Al-Bouti, p. 299.

practiced only by the hard-hearted who have no God. How can a man with such teachings call himself the prophet of God?

The Right to Kill

The fanaticism of Muhammad was not limited to his discrimination in favor of his daughter, Fatima. Muhammad also made it lawful for a brother to kill his brother, or a father to kill his son, or a son to kill his father during a battle to spread Islam. A son can kill his father if the father does not embrace Islam. That made it legal to kill a disbelieving relative or friend. However, this law was *not* applicable to the relatives of Muhammad!

This illogical discrimination was recorded in more than one Islamic reference, including *The Life of Prophet* by Ibn Hisham, who wrote:

> "Ibn Ishaq said, Ibn Abbas said that the Prophet said to his companions during the Battle of Badr:[86] Whoever of you finds someone of the children of Hashem, you should not kill him; and whoever finds my uncle, Al-Abbas, you should not kill him. Hudhayfah[87] said to him: Do we then kill our sons, our fathers, our uncles and our kinfolk but we let alone Al-Abbas because he is your uncle? Umar almost killed him because he dared to confront the Prophet of Allah."[88]

Hudhayfah was one of Muhammad's close companions,

---

86) The Battle of Badr was fought on March 17, 624.
87) Hudhayfah Ibn al-Yaman (died in 656).
88) The *Hadith* said only those at the Battle of Badr who became Muslims could be spared. This is why Hudhayfah was angry! See the *Hadith* of Sahih Bukhari, Vol. 5, Book 59, #354; Vol. 9, Book 83, #5; and the *Hadith* of Sahih Muslim, Book 1, #173-175.

but he refused to accept oppression and discrimination – even by Muhammad. After Hudhayfah confronted Muhammad on the matter, Muhammad complained to Umar Ibn al-Khattab:

> "Should the uncle of the Prophet of Allah be killed by the sword?"

What kind of strange logic was that? Was not his uncle an *unbeliever* like all the unbelievers? Were not his family unbelievers like all the unbelievers in Quraish, his own tribe, who were killed without mercy by their sons, fathers, relatives and friends?

During the Battle of Uhud,[89] Al-Shayma', Muhammad's foster sister, was taken captive. However, she was not treated like the rest of the unbelieving captives, who were enslaved by the Muslims, in accordance with Muslim laws. When Muhammad was told that his sister was among the captives, he treated her well and offered her the choice to go back to her home or stay with him in honor. She chose to leave, and left with honor, carrying many presents.[90]

Double Standards

The greatest story of Muhammad's discrimination and double standards is reflected in his statement: "Succession after me should be vested only in Quraish."[91]

Muhammad's confederates, who came from outside Quraish, were his best supporters during his calling. Sa'd Ibn

---

89) Fought on March 23, 625 at Uhud, near Medina.

90) See *Al-Kamel fi al-Tarikh (The Perfect in History)* by Ibn Al-Athir, Vol. 2, p. 179; and *Rawd Al-Unuf* by As-Suhaili, Vol. IV, p. 130.

91) See the *Hadith* of Sahih Bukhari, Vol. 4, Book 56, #704-705; Vol. 9, Book 89, #254 & 329; as well as the *Hadith* of Sahih Muslim, Book 20, Chapter 1 "The People Are Subservient to the Quraish and the Caliphate is the Right of the Quraish," #4473-4484.

Ubadah was first on the list of Muhammad's successors because he received him at Medina, and called Muhammad's
people to accept and support him. Had it not been for Sa'd,
Muhammad's calling would have totally failed. Despite that,
Muhammad ordered the succession to stay in his Quraish
tribe. Although the people of Quraish persecuted him and
declared war against him, he gave them, not his allies (the
Ansars), the right to succeed him.

After his death, Muhammad's relatives insisted that the
succession, i.e. the Caliphate, should stay in Quraish. The
Ansars were not considered because they were not from the
Quraish tribe. Bitter fights broke out on the very day Muhammad died because the first candidate in line to succeed
him was Sa'd Ibn Ubadah of the Ansars.

Al-Suyuti said,

> "Muhammad said, The leadership and the caliphate
> after me should stay in Quraish."[92]

To which Al-Bukhari added:

> "The Messenger of Allah said, The government and
> the caliphate should stay in Quraish, even if two
> survivors of them remained."[93]

That was *said* by Muhammad and was confirmed by Muslim scholars. What about when Muhammad said:

> "No preference to an Arab over a foreigner except
> in piety"?

In this statement, Muhammad made the Arabs equal to
non-Arabs; and further, he supposed to have preferred the

---

92) *The History of the Caliphs* by Al-Suyuti, p. 10.
93) See the *Hadith* of Sahih Bukhari, Vol. 4, Book 56, #705 and Vol. 9,
Book 89, #254.

non-Arab to the non-pious Arab.[94] His decision to hand the Caliphate over to the Quraish tribe is absolute hypocrisy! Ali bin Abu Talib was quoted by Ibn Kathir:

"The Messenger of Allah preferred Quraish over the rest of the world."[95]

Was that justice on the part of the Messenger of Allah? Why these clear contradictions in his words and deeds? Why were his kinfolk the preferred ones? Could Muhammad be a chosen prophet of Allah, yet say and do such things? This is far from God, the One who commands justice, no matter the conditions. Maybe Muhammad's logic can prevail under ages of oppression and racism. Such racist logic may prevail within the borders of Satan's domain to this day, but it has no place within the Kingdom of the true, just God.

Muhammad was not satisfied by restricting the succession of the Caliphate to the people of Quraish. He also practiced discrimination at the time of the distribution of the booty. Muhammad gave more of the spoils to non-Muslim Quraishis than to Muslims not from the tribe of Quraish!

Sheikh Abu Sa'id Al-Khudri related:

"The Prophet, after the Battle of Hunein,[96] gave of much of the booty to people whose faith in Islam was weak, in order to bring them closer; and he gave the same to some who did not embrace Islam,

---

94) This comes from what is called Muhammad's *Farewell Address*: "O people! Verily your Lord is one and your father is one. All of you belong to one ancestry of Adam and Adam was created out of clay. There is no superiority for an Arab over a non-Arab and for a non-Arab over an Arab; nor for white over the black nor for the black over the white except in piety. Verily the noblest among you is he who is the most pious."
95) *The Beginning and the End* by Ismail Ibn Kathir, p. 171.
96) The Battle of Hunein (or Hunain) was fought in 630, mentioned in the Qur'an in Sura *At-Tauba* (Repentance) 9:25-26.

such as Safwan bin Ubia,[97] to entice them into Islam. When Muhammad behaved this way, giving to non-Muslims more than to the Muslim allies who fought with him and supported him, they became angry. One said: 'Is this justice, Muhammad? I cannot see Allah's face in this distribution.' Muhammad was infuriated and his face turned red with anger. He answered: 'Woe to you! Who can be fair if I am not fair?' The man answered him: 'Where is justice in what you are doing?' That confrontation took place in the presence of Khalid and Umar, who tried to waste the man, but Muhammad stopped them because he was afraid to lose the backing of the allies (Al-Ansar). However, he asked Sa'd Ibn Ubadah, the chief of the Al-Ansar, to take care of the 'rude' man. Sa'd answered: 'Be fair Muhammad. I stand behind the man and his statement that you are not fair.'"[98]

Dr. Al-Bouti wrote:

"The Prophet favored the people of Mecca with more spoils than others of his supporters, and he did not respect the principle of genuine equality among warriors."[99]

Earlier in the same book we learn that the Al-Ansar objected and said: "May Allah forgive His Prophet."[100] That is, if he *were* a prophet!

Muhammad was disturbed greatly by the unequal division and distribution of the spoils because he wanted to re-

97) That is, Safwan bin Umayya. See the *Hadith* of Sahih Muslim, Book 30, #5730 and *Malik's Muwatta*, Book 28, #28.20.44.

98) *The Light of Certainty* (Nur Al-Yaqin), 24th edition, pp. 235-237.

99) *The Jurisprudence of the Life of Muhammad*, p. 603.

100) *The Jurisprudence of the Life of Muhammad*, p. 301.

gain the people's favor and full support. What did he do? Of course, "Gabriel" immediately brought down a verse from his god, without reprimanding Muhammad, to relieve him of any wrongdoing – showing that Allah supported Muhammad's injustices.

Hassan bin Thabit, who was a strong supporter of Muhammad and wrote poems endorsing him, criticized Muhammad describing him as unfair and unjust. Ibn Hisham recorded some of those lines of poetry in his book.[101] Muhammad's stand of unfairness and injustice was repeated many times, and you can read about it in many of the Islamic references.[102]

As a result of deeper research into these matters, Dr. Taha Hussein,[103] a great Egyptian author, wrote his well-known book, *The Grand Revolt*; then left Islam and embraced Christianity. He was baptized in a church in France.[104]

Post-Mortum Orders

A great injustice of Muhammad, which is egotism beyond compare, was his commanded to all Muslims never to marry his wives after he died. How did this come about? One day he saw his wife Aisha speaking with a young man named

101) *The Jurisprudence of the Life of Muhammad*, Vol. IV, pp. 71-72.
102) See *The Life of Muhammad* by Dr. Haikal, pp. 441-442; *The Beginning and the End* by Ibn Kathir, Vol. IV, p. 353; *Jawami' Al-Sira* by Ibn Hazm, p. 159; *Rawd Al-Unuf* by As-Suhaili, Vol. IV, pp. 156-157; *Al-Sira Al-Halabia* by Al-Halabi, Vol. III, pp, 85-97; and *History of Nations and Kings* by Al-Tabari, Vol. II, pp. 175-76.
103) Taha Hussein Ph.D. (1889-1973), known as *A'meed al-Adab al-A'raby*, "the Dean of Arabic Literature."
104) This was confirmed in *Taha Hussein in the Intellectual Balance* by Dr. Anwar Gundi, p. 65 and affirmed in an article published in the intellectual *Renaissance* magazine by Muhammad Mahmood, a lawyer and known Egyptian writer.

Talha, Aisha's cousin. Talha was upset, and said: "Does Muhammad marry our wives, but forbid us from talking to our cousins?"

When Aisha, Hafsa, and Zainab heard about Muhammad's orders, they revolted against him. They could not accept that Muhammad told people that his wives could not remarry after his death. Consequently, they demanded a divorce so that when he died, they would not be bound by his order. Then Aisha, Hafsa, and Zainab left their homes and refused to return until Muhammad amended his decision.

Muhammad found himself in a great predicament. How could he get out of it? The solution was once again ever present. "Gabriel" brought down a verse that reprimanded Talha and supported Muhammad's stand. The verse says:

> "Nor is it right for you that ye should annoy Allah's Messenger, or that ye should marry his widows after him at any time."[105]

Again, Muhammad's god rescued him from his predicament. After a seizure and a tantrum with snoring, foaming and passing out, Muhammad woke up to say: "I got a verse." And he had many more where they came from!

Muhammad died only six months after that incident. Aisha was eighteen years old, Safiya was twenty, and most of his other wives were hardly passed their twenties. Could God have commanded this continued injustice after Muhammad's death? Was it not enough for Aisha to marry Muhammad at nine when he was fifty-four? Then she had to live a life of deprivation for the rest of his life.

What about Safiya, who was coerced to marry Muhammad at the age of seventeen, after her young, newly-wed-

---

105) Sura *Al-Ahzab* (the Allies) 33:53.

ded husband was murdered by Muhammad's men, and then made a widow again at the age of twenty?

What kind of a god would order such instructions? Wasn't the grief of these women enough, having to endure all that deprivation during the life of Muhammad? And now even more after his death? Could that man be a prophet of God? What kind of a god would send to us a Messenger such as Muhammad, with such a character? Surely such a god is of Muhammad's own making.

Further Injustices Following Muhammad's Death

The legislation of Islamic countries in general agrees with Muhammad and his Qur'anic teaching on discrimination against women. For example, one man's share of inheritance is equal to two women's shares; and one man's testimony in a court of law is equal to the testimony of two women.

Also, according to the Qur'an, it is lawful for a husband to beat up a woman when necessary. The Qur'an has extinguished women's rights and treats them as a commodity to be sold and bought, like a doll that can be beaten, abandoned, thrown out or forcibly married to another when she is already married. The more you study Islam, the clearer you will see that Muhammad and the code of Islamic justice is by no means just.

4

Terrorism and Intimidation in Islam

In this chapter, we will discuss the raids and battles of Muslims under the leadership of Muhammad and his successors, the Caliphs. Also, we will discuss the unlimited cruelty of this supposed man of mercy and compassion.

He was more racist than any of his companions, and he boasted about it on more than one occasion. By this he was reflecting an inferiority complex that he suffered all of his life – namely, because he endured dire poverty until the age of twenty-five, coupled with being unlearned.

To counter his past, he gave himself wealth, prestige, and prophethood. But where did this poor, unlearned man who grew up at his poor uncle's house get all this wealth?

Life after Khadija

The first good deal in Muhammad's life was his marriage to Khadija bint Khuwaylid, who inherited the wealth of her late husband and his family. When she died, Muhammad was her sole heir. That was the beginning of Muhammad's riches. When his calling to prophethood became apparent, Muhammad *needed* great wealth to spread around to the poor people and slaves who were his first followers, to whom he also promised freedom and money.

In this way Muhammad formed the first nucleus of his calling while he was still in Mecca. However, the people of Mecca and Quraish, his own tribe, were not convinced of his calling. When his speeches and teachings became unbearable to the people of Mecca, they declared war against him and planned to kill him. Muhammad managed to escape from Mecca and seek refuge in Medina, the city of his supporters (whom he called *Al-Ansar*), most of whom received and backed him. In Medina, he doubled the number of his followers to sixty men. But now he faced a problem. Where would he get all the money he needed to spend on all those men? He could find no other way than to conduct raids and robberies, resulting in murder and spilling of blood.

The First Four Raids

The caravans of Mecca passed by Medina on their way to and from Damascus, full of merchandise and goods. Muhammad and his gang would set an ambush for them, quickly robbing and killing the merchants. It is regrettable that the first job Muhammad, the spiritual leader of his group, had in Medina was robbing caravans and killing merchants.

His first raid was known as the raid of **Al-Iwa'**, where he assaulted a camel caravan that belonged to some Quraishis.[106]

The second raid was known as **Bawat**, where he assaulted a caravan from Mecca led by Umia bin Khalaf, which he succeeded in robbing.

In the third raid, known as **Al-Ashira**, a caravan going to Damascus was assaulted by Muhammad and his gang with

---

106) See *The Life of the Messenger* by Imam Muhammad bin Abd Al-Wahab, p. 85.

the intent to rob it only, but they ended up killing five of its men during the course of the robbery.

The fourth raid was known as **Al-Nakhla**, a place between Mecca and Taif. Muhammad's lieutenant, Abd Allah bin Jahsh, led twelve men in an assault on a caravan carrying mainly raisins and cloths. It was led by Amr bin Al-Hadrami, who was killed in the Prohibited Month, the month in which Islam prohibited killing and fighting. But to Muhammad, such prohibition was only on paper, with no real meaning.

Muhammad, as always, found justification for his dilemma, as it came down upon him in the following verse:

> "They ask thee concerning fighting in the prohibited
> month. Say: "Fighting therein is a grave (offense);
> but graver is it in the sight of Allah to prevent access
> to the path of Allah ...."[107]

The agreement between Muhammad and his gang was that he got 20% of the loot and the men got 80%. As a result of those raids, Muhammad and his men accumulated a huge amount of capital. With it they financed a greater number of men, who performed bigger jobs.

Consequently, the great Battle of Badr took place on the day of Farkan in the month of Ramadan.[108] Muhammad was told that many camels loaded with goods were going from Damascus to Mecca, led by Abu Sufyan (the wealthiest man in Mecca). Muhammad, with three hundred men, went out to rob it. Abu Sufyan was told of Muhammad's plan, so he sent to Mecca asking for their help to rescue their assets.

Muhammad mobilized his supporters (Al-Ansar) under

---

107) Sura *Al-Baqara* (the Cow) 2:217.
108) March 17, 624 AD, or "17 Ramadan, 2 AH" (2 years *After* the *Hijra*) in the Islamic calendar.

the leadership of Sa'd Ibn Mua'dh. Al-Miqdad bin Al-As-wad said to Muhammad,

> "We (Al-Ansar who joined Muhammad at Medina) will have of the spoil the same share as the emigrants (those who fled with Muhammad from Mecca to Medina), and Muhammad will have the fifth. Lead us therefore, and we will not say as the people of Moses said to him: Go, you and your Lord, and fight, while we stay here."

That last statement by Al-Miqdad became a verse in the Qur'an![109]

Muhammad was satisfied with the accord between the Al-Ansar and the Emigrants and was quoted by reliable sources, saying:

> "March and rejoice, for Allah has promised me one of two denominations and I see the slain of the people."

As usual, "Gabriel" came down upon Muhammad with the needed verse:

> "I will instill terror into the hearts of the Unbelievers; smite ye above their necks, and smite all their finger-tips off them."[110]

Then another verse was sent down:

> "I promise you a thousand angels ready to fight for you."[111]

The tribe of Quraish attempted to return to Mecca, but found it difficult to fight their brethren and relatives who were on Muhammad's side. But Muhammad made sure his

---

109) See Sura *Al-Ma'idah* (the Table Spread, or the Food) 5:24.

110) Sura *Al-Anfal* (the Spoils of War) 8:12.

111) In Sura *Al-Imran* (the Family of Imran) 3:124, *3,000* angels were promised at the Battle of Badr!

followers were turned into the enemies of their own brethren. Amer bin Al-Hadrami, son of Umar Al-Hadrami, who became a follower of Muhammad, met his brother in the battle and cried: "O, Umar, O, my brother!" But Muhammad ordered him killed.

Consequently, the Battle of Badr started. It resulted in the death of more than four hundred men from Mecca, including Abu-Al-Hakam, Muhammad's own uncle.

When the news came to Muhammad, he demanded to see his uncle's corpse. When he saw him, he spit on his face and said: "This is the Pharaoh of this nation."

Muhammad left to divide the spoils of the war among himself and his men. But after the spoils were divided, Muhammad killed Al-Nadr bin Al-Harith. And when he came to Al-Zabia, he killed Akaba bin Abi Abita.

As Muhammad came to Medina, he ordered the spoils to be gathered:

> "Who was the one who defeated them? Therefore they are mine. Who would have defeated Quraish? Without me, there would have been no spoils."

As usual, Muhammad solved that problem with a verse that came down upon him:

> "They ask you about the spoils, you say, the spoils are for Allah and His Messenger."[112]

Thus Muhammad usurped all the spoils. [113]

The Battle of Badr[114]

Who began the aggression of the Battle of Badr? Was it

---

112) Sura *Al-Anfal* (the Spoils of War) 8:11.

113) This is how the battle was recorded in *The Brief of the Life of the Prophet Muhammad* by Muhammad bin Abd Al-Wahab, pp. 91-92.

114) The Battle of Badr was fought on March 17, 624.

the people of Quraish, or was it Muhammad and his followers? The caravan was coming back from Damascus to Mecca, led by Abu Sufyan, when Muhammad came to rob it and kill its guards. Was that not blatant aggression? Did God order Muhammad to kill and rob? What god orders such atrocities?

Those who were killed in that battle were numerous, but that did not satisfy Muhammad. So he had to entertain himself on the way by killing captives. As he began his way back, he killed Al-Nadr bin Al-Harith, and when he came closer to the gates of the city, he killed Akaba bin Abi Al-Mu'ait. Could there be more terrorism than the Prophet killing people for entertainment?

When Sa'd Ibn Mua'dh criticized what the men were doing as they were killing the captives, Muhammad said to him, "You seem to hate what the men are doing." He answered him, "Yes. Killing captives is not an Arab tradition." Muhammad answered, "But these were unbelievers." Mua'dh answered, "They could have become Muslims if we talked to them nicely." Then he said to Muhammad his famous statement: "As though the exaggeration in killing is more favorable to you than keeping those men alive."

The strangest thing that happened in this battle was the death of Muhammad's uncle Abu Al-Hakam (meaning man of wisdom), to whom Muslims refer as Abu Al-Jahl (man of ignorance). He refused to kill Muhammad when he had the chance during the battle, saying, "How can I kill my nephew, the son of my brother Abd Allah." That was the stance of one that the Muslims refer to as "man of ignorance." But the stance of Muhammad and his followers toward his uncle was totally different. Muhammad bin Abd Al-Wahab said in his book:

"When the war cooled down, and the foe was defeated, the Messenger of Allah said, 'Who would
find what happened to Abu Jahl (in the battle)?'
Ibn Mas'ud went to find that he was wounded, but
Ibn Mas'ud and Awfa bin Afra' beat him up, and
they said to him, 'Who is defeated now?' When he
did not answer, Ibn Mas'ud beheaded him with his
sword. But before he was killed, he said, 'Can a man
who was killed by his own kinfolk be defeated?' Ibn
Mas'ud beheaded him while he was deeply wounded. Then he went to Muhammad and told him that
he killed him. Muhammad said, 'Go and show him
to me.' When Muhammad saw his uncle, he spit
at him and said, 'The pharaoh of this nation has
died.'"[115]

Some of those who were taken captive in that battle were
Abd Al-Rahman bin Awf, Umayya bin Khalaf and his son
Ali. Balal, who was a bond-slave in Umayya's house, saw
them. But when Balal became one of Muhammad's followers, Umayya chastised him, but he did not kill him. However, Balal insisted that the two captives, Umayya and his
son, must be killed by the sword, even though they begged
for their lives.

What cruelty! Is that what religion does? How can we
compare their faith and action with Christ, who said:

"Love your enemy, bless them that curse you."[116]

Where was the forgiveness Islam claims to propagate?

If we analyze the Battle of Badr (which Muslim scholars
consider a military conquest), we find that it was not a war as

115) *The Brief of the Life of the Messenger* by Imam Muhammad bin Abd
Al-Wahab (edition published in Saudi Arabia), p. 91.
116) Matthew 5:44

we understand war. Muhammad's intention was not fighting and killing unbelievers, but robbing a rich caravan. The story began when Abu Sufyan was informed of Muhammad's intention, and he sent asking for the support of the people of Mecca to come and foil a robbery attempt by "Ali Baba and the forty thieves." The victory was not as Muslims claim it to be: "A genius military victory."

The main question here is: Does a prophet's calling depend on thieving and robbing people? Regrettably, Muslims learned their lessons from the founder of their religion. For this reason, much killing, murdering and oppression have been committed on a wide scale by Muslims. They have made it legal to kill the infidel Christians and Jews wherever they find them (whenever they can get away with it), as they are doing in Egypt and many other Muslim countries.

Don't forget that their religion was founded on robbing, raiding and invading – and had *nothing* to do with love, mercy and compassion. Under which law can captives be killed or beaten as though they are animals? How could Muhammad be called the prophet of mercy, when the wine he drank after every battle was the blood of the innocent?

Then Muhammad received ready-made declarations from his god to open wide the doors for him in that field:

> "O my Lord, Leave not of the Unbelievers, a single one on earth."[117]

The main purpose behind Muhammad's raids and invasions was to gain wealth and acquire beautiful women. After the Battle of Badr, Muhammad took seventy women captive. Abu Bakr suggested he free them, so that Allah would guide them to become believers on Muhammad and his call-

---

117) Sura *Nuh* (Noah) 71:26.

ing. But Muhammad did not care about his calling as much
as he cared about accumulating his wealth. His calling was
nothing more than a cover for his greed. And of course, the
god of Muhammad was ready, and "Gabriel" was very quick
to bring down *the verses that would justify Muhammad's
actions, as in this verse:*

> "Therefore, when ye meet the Unbelievers (in
> fight), smite at their necks; At length, when ye have
> thoroughly subdued them, bind a bond firmly (on
> them): thereafter (is the time for) either generosity
> or ransom: Until the war lays down its burdens."[118]

The bargaining began between the people of Mecca and
the Muslims to ransom each prisoner. Consequently, the
Quraishis sold their homes and households and gave the
money to Muhammad to redeem their captives.

Muhammad ambushed the Quraishi caravan, and surprised them when they were not expecting a battle. The men
who were in the caravan were mere merchants, carrying their
goods back from Damascus to Mecca. Those men and their
employed workers attempted to protect their wealth against
the highway bandits that came to rob them.

The Battle of Uhud[119]

Soon after the robbery of Badr, Quraish decided to avenge
the raid against Muhammad and his followers. As soon as
Abu Sufyan arrived in Mecca, he gathered its masters and
they decided to launch a war against Muhammad and his
band. A three-thousand-man army was mobilized, and they
marched towards Medina. They camped near Mount Uhud,
readying themselves to attack the city. Muhammad was told
of the army mobilized against Medina, and he was afraid

118) Sura *Muhammad* 47:4.
119) The Battle of Uhud was fought on March 23, 625.

to go out to fight them. He thought it was better to attack them in the town from the rooftops as they entered the city. Abd Allah bin Ubai agreed with him. Al-Ansar, the people of Medina, feared for their city, their women and their children; therefore they insisted that Muhammad should go outside the city to fight them. They told him that if disaster ensued against him in the battle, it would be better than a disaster inside the city.

Muhammad's band called upon his god to come down and fight for them. The Muslims were made to believe that with Allah and his angels standing for them, the victory would surely be theirs. (But Muhammad knew within himself that neither Allah nor his angels would be there for him.) Regardless, he said to his followers, "I will ask Allah and His angels to fight for us." One thousand of his men went out to fight with the promise that thousands of angels would fight beside them. The battle began, but suddenly the "angels" of Muhammad were defeated and the followers retreated with fear. "Gabriel" must have been on a very important mission somewhere else. In the end, only five men came back, defeated and fleeing from Quraish.

Muhammad tried to come up with a convincing explanation for the humiliation of the Battle of Uhud. People asked: Where was the god of Muhammad? Where were the twenty thousand angels that Muhammad promised would fight for them? "Where were they, Muhammad?" shouted Sa'd Ben, who was deeply wounded during the battle. The founders of Islam gathered around their leader and asked him: "Abu Kasem (that was the name his companions called him), what are we going to do? Now Al-Ansar (the allies) will never believe us anymore."

Muhammad asked his men for some time to come up with

an answer. However, the opportunity Muhammad needed was clear, for he knew the answer to their question. "Gabriel" was ready. But Al-Ansar would not be convinced this time by one verse, so, *sixty-one* verses came down that became a part of the Sura![120] (They were not convinced until the sixty-first verse came down.) Also, Muhammad made more than four hundred other statements, which were recorded in the *Ahadith*[121] of Sahih Bukhari and Sahih Muslim.

After the Battle of Uhud, Muhammad and his companions had to take a closer look at what had caused them to lose 70% of everything that they built up throughout the past years. So they decided to return to the guaranteed looting raids after they executed a truce with Quraish for ten years. That truce gave Muhammad enough time to restore the prestige he lost, by looting the wealth and the weapons of traveling caravans. In the fourth year of Hijra[122], he successfully assaulted Dabeeb and BerMa'ouna. During the last month of that year, Muhammad decided to assault some wealthy people, the people of Al-Nadir (known as the *Banu Nadir*). He raided them, then took their wealth and their women. Of course, what was done to the people of Al-Nadir became lawful for Muslims, i.e., robbing unbelievers and raping and taking their wives captives.

Because Al-Ansar complained about what he did to Al-Nadir, Sura 59, *Al-Hashr* (the Exile) came down to put an end to all disputes. It seems his god became so generous with him that he did not send him just *one* verse as before, but now *a whole Sura* came down to justify his actions!

---

120) Sura *Al-Imran* (the Family of Imran) 3:121-181.

121) *Ahadith* is the plural form of *Hadith*.

122) *The fourth year of Hijra*. That is, 626 (four years after the Hijra, Muhammad's flight from Medina to Mecca).

The Raid against al-Muraisa

In the fifth year of Hijra, the raid against Al-Muraisa took place. But during that raid more took place than killing, robbing and taking captives. The people of Mustaliq fled from the raiders, but the Muslims pursued them and captured their cattle, their camels, and much spoil besides taking their women as captives.

During that raid, two exciting stories provoked many questions and debates among learned Muslims. One of those two stories still provokes many questions among the well-educated Muslims; i.e., the story of Aisha, the spoiled wife of Muhammad, with Safwan bin Al-Mu'attal.

These two stories will be told as they happened. It will raise questions for you about how realistic contemporary Muslim thinking was. Muslim writers told those stories as they happened in the fifth year of Hijra, when Muhammad was almost sixty years old, and Aisha was fifteen.

The Story of Aisha and Safwan

It was known that Muhammad consummated his marriage with Aisha when she was nine. At that age, a young girl does not recognize completely what is happening to her, sexually. Besides, she did not have those mature feelings that differentiate between one man and another and to which direction her feelings should go.

However, as Aisha grew older, her feelings also matured. But in which direction were her feelings going? It seems that at the time of the raid against Al-Miraysi, Muhammad did not have the patience to wait until he returned home, but he asked Aisha to accompany him. In other words, while his men were assailing, robbing and stealing, he was in his tent with Aisha.

However, this time, Aisha did not answer the insults and

wounds Muhammad gave her and other women, except by putting him in front of his people in a very embarrassing situation. As you read the following, ask yourself: why was Aisha's answer necessary?

When the companions of Muhammad took the women of Al-Mustaliq clan, they displayed to him the captive women. Among these was Juwayriyyah bint Al-Harith, who was very beautiful, and Muhammad wanted to marry her. But because she was a part of the spoils of Thabit bin Qais, Muhammad offered him much money to buy her for himself, and he married her. That transaction took place even as Aisha was with him in the tent during that raid.

What was Aisha's response? Aisha left her camel palanquin as the group approached the city, and she entered into one of the deserted houses. After seven hours, she came back with Safwan bin Al-Mu'attal,[123] with many people seeing them entering into Medina.

As the gossip spread about Aisha and Safwan, Muhammad was sure that she betrayed him, so he sought the advice of Ali. Ali's advice for him was either to divorce her or to kill her. Muhammad decided to divorce her, and Ali expected that Muhammad would act on his decision. However, a full month passed, while people were still talking about the affair of Safwan and Aisha, but Muhammad did not divorce her or take a stand towards her. Ali repeated his counsel on the matter, and Muhammad answered, I will go now to her father's house to divorce her. He actually went there for the purpose of divorcing her. He entered into the house of Abu Bakr, and as soon as he saw Aisha, he changed his mind, and he said to her, "O Aisha, Allah has vindicated you." Of course, "Gabriel" was as ready as ever, and his god was able

123) Also known as Safwan bin Mu'attal As-Sulami Adh-Dhakwani.

to send him a verse to meet the need. Thus, that problem was solved by a verse that testified for the vindication of Aisha.[124]

A short time later, Ali saw a recurring impropriety of Aisha, so he told Muhammad. This time Muhammad decided that Aisha should be killed. He went to her with Ali, and with his sword, ready to kill her. Muhammad entered the house while Ali waited outside, but Muhammad came out after about one hour, sweating and exhausted. Ali asked him: "Did you kill her, Cousin?" Muhammad answered, "No, Ali. A verse came down from Allah to vindicate her again." But this time, the verse accused Ali of lying, saying those who came with the gossip were "a band from your midst."[125]

From that day on, Ali stood against Aisha, and Aisha was antagonistic towards Ali, who was the preacher of good tidings about Paradise, sent by Muhammad as one of the Ten Preachers. Muhammad said about Ali, "He is my cousin and my brother who ransomed me. He is Truthfulness, he is Ali bin Abu Talib." But the god of Muhammad turned around and accused him of lying in the episode of Aisha.

The Sura of Succession[126]

That family feud between Muhammad and Ali resulted in Muhammad deleting the Sura of Succession that intended

---

124) This story, from Aisha's own point of view, is told in the *Hadith* of Sahih Bukhari, Vol. 3, Book 48, #805, 829; Vol. 5, Book 59, #462-464; and Vol. 6, Book 60, #274-278.
125) For the full "revelation" see Sura *Al-Nur* (the Light) 24:1-26.
126) The Sura of Succession (omitted from every Sunni Qur'an) is in every Shiite Qur'an, consisting of five verses: "In the name of Allah, the merciful, the compassionate. 1. O ye who believe! Believe on the prophet and the Protector. 2. Who is one from the other. 3. And I am who hears and knows. 4. Those who believed and did the good deeds will have the joy of paradise. 5. Praise the glory of thy Lord, ***and Ali is one of the witnesses***" (emphasis mine).

to give the caliphate to Ali. Please note: the backers of Ali (the Shiites) have insisted on the existence of the Sura of Succession and recite it from their Qur'an even to this day.

When Caliph 'Uthman gathered the Qur'an, he refused to include that Sura, and insisted on deleting it. But it was included in Ibn Mas'oud's copy of the Qur'an, and it is in the Qur'an that is read by Iranians and all the Shiites in general. They number about 40% of all Muslims. Therefore, the Qur'an that is read by the Shiites has 115 suras, while the Qur'an that is read by the Sunnis has 114 suras. This discrepancy is the result of the important strife that took place after the raid of Muraisa, in the fifth year of Hijra.

The Foundation of Terrorism

This event is similar to the incidence of Muhammad's marriage to Juwayriyyah bint Al-Harith, after he killed her captive father and husband. It also shows Muhammad's extreme cruelty in marrying women after killing fathers and husbands. Aisha responded to Muhammad's behavior by betraying him as was cited above.[127] Here, I cannot but ask the traditional question: Was that the behavior of a prophet who was sent by God?

It is clear that Islam rose upon the foundation of terrorism. It began by raiding, killing, stealing and robbing the caravans of Quraish who were coming from Damascus to Mecca. It went on to assaulting the Jews, whether at Khaybar or at Medina, and the Christians at Medina and Taif. Muslims throughout history have followed in the steps of the founder of the Islamic religion, Muhammad bin Abd Allah. Because of that, today we see Islamists in Egypt rob the stores and churches of Christians, killing them without

---

127) This story comes from *The Life of the Prophet* by Muhammad bin Abd Al-Wahab, pp. 101-102.

any remorse. Why shouldn't they do that when their prophet, Muhammad, led in those detestable actions during his raids and assaults, allowing the killing of the innocent, stealing their wealth, and raping their captive wives?

His acts of terrorism and intimidation were documented in the best Islamic biographies of Muhammad. [128]

In Algeria, fanatic Muslims have been killing innocent people, both Muslims and non-Muslims, with no questions asked, just because they oppose their political and religious agenda, or because they are loyal to the government. People must understand that Muhammad has been the example of the Muslims in the East and the West. When Muslims read his story, they want to emulate it in every aspect.

The Raid against the Jews of Mustala

In the same year was the raid of the Muraisa against the Jewish people of Mustala, who suffered torture and killing under Muhammad. Many of those Jews fled to Mecca, seeking the help of the Quraish, with whom they had treaties and covenants of friendship and cooperation. They met Abu Sufyan, who became the leader of Quraish and all those who were hurt by the raids of Muhammad.

The renewal of the treaty between the Jews and the Quraish was completed and signed by Salam bin Al-Haqiq for the Jews, and Abu Sufyan for Mecca. (Some Muslim historians record that the Jews betrayed their promises to Muhammad. But our Muslim friends earnestly wanted to turn the truth upside-down so they presented totally false claims. For *Muhammad* was the one who betrayed the Jews, raiding their caravans and towns and killing them.)

---

128) See, for instance, the *Hadith* of Sahih Bukhari, *The Causes of Descendancy*, by Al-Suyuti, *The Life of the Prophet* by Muhammad bin Abd Al-Wahab and other authoritative references.

The Battle of the Trench[129]

Because of all these raids by Muhammad, Abu Sufyan led four thousand men of his tribe against him. When Muhammad heard the news, his companions asked him: "Shall the angels fight for us, O Messenger of Allah?" But Salman the Persian said to him, "O Messenger of Allah, they fought for us in the Battle of Uhud, and you know the result. We were totally defeated. Why didn't Allah and his angels give us the victory?" Muhammad did not answer, so Salman said, "Let us dig trenches that would separate between us, the city and the enemy." Muhammad accepted the suggestion immediately, and he himself began to dig.

After digging the trench, Muhammad sent three thousand men, led by Huyay bin Akhtab, to besiege the fort of Banu Quraiza. Huyay asked Ka'eb bin Asad, the leader of Banu Quraiza, to open the fort, promising him that they would be safe. The number of Banu Quraiza's men was between nine hundred and one thousand. Those men trusted Huyay and surrendered their arms. Huyay led them to Muhammad, who ordered them imprisoned until he made a decision in their case. His final decision against those nine hundred men was the sentence of death. Then he divided their women and children between his companions. The reason for their killing was that, while they were besieged for twenty-five days, Ali heard them cursing Muhammad. For this reason, when they were brought to Muhammad, he came close to them and said, "You curse me, you brothers of pigs and monkeys?" For that, their punishment was death.

Where was that prophet from Jesus Christ who said: "Love your enemies and bless them that curse you"? Muhammad bin Abd Allah, the Messenger of mercy, cursed

129) The Battle of the Trench was fought against Medina in 627.

and killed those who cursed him. He even practiced collective punishment against men, from young to old. Could that be logical or be of God? Where was mercy, O Prophet of mercy and justice?

The Muslims made a treaty with the Jews on that day, promising that they would not be touched with any harm if they only surrendered their weapons and pay the tributes. For this reason, Banu Quraiza surrendered themselves and their weapons to Muhammad. But Muhammad did not honor the treaty and ordered them killed.

Before I tell what happened to the women and the children, I have to mention that Muhammad asked for Sa'd Ibn Mua'dh's opinion about killing the nine hundred men. Mua'dh consented. It is intriguing that after Mua'dh gave his consent, he was immediately stricken with a fatal heart attack.

After Mua'dh's death, Muhammad declared that "Gabriel" told him that the gates of heaven were wide open for Mua'dh, and that the Throne of Allah shook at his death. The angels rejoiced by his spirit, and seventy thousand of them came down to attend his funeral. Can you believe that statement, Muhammad said that his god welcomed into his paradise a man that consented to the murder of nine hundred innocent men, young and old. What kind of a butcher was his god?

Muhammad ordered that those men be brought, ten at a time, to be beheaded, thrown into a ditch, and covered with dirt. During the carnage, their women screamed, tore their clothes and beat on their cheeks. Muhammad continued the slaughter. The more the women wailed, the more he and his companions were determined to finish the butchering, until, in that day, he butchered nine hundred men.

While Muhammad's hands were still stained and his clothes soaked with the blood of Banu Quraiza's men, Muhammad demanded that the captive women be displayed in his presence. As usual, Muhammad chose for himself the most beautiful woman, one whose husband, three brothers and all her family were ordered to be killed by him in front of her eyes. Her name was Rihana bint Amro. Muhammad said to her, "Instead of becoming my slave, I will free you and marry you." She answered him:

> "It is more honorable for me to be your slave than to be the wife of a butcher of men."

Then she spit at him, hoping that he would order her killed. But Muhammad did not kill beautiful women. Instead, he kept her as a slave and had intercourse with her while her hands and legs were tied.[130]

What god would send a prophet whose clothes were still soaked by the blood of nine hundred victims, when he seeks sexual intercourse with a woman who preferred slavery and death to being "the wife of a butcher of men," as she described him? My heart bleeds for my people who are still following behind that man, and they repeatedly refer to him as a prophet and a Messenger of God. All my people need to do is to read the story of his life so that they can understand what I say – I hope!

The Jews have inherited hatred for the followers of Muhammad since that time, and they still remember how much

---

130) See also *The Life of the Prophet* by Ibn Hisham, Vol. III, pp. 118-143 (who includes other events not listed here); *The Life of Muhammad* by Haikal, pp. 347-351 (who added more details of Muhammad's cruelty); and *Al-Sira Al-Halabia* by Al-Halabi, Vol. II, pp. 675-677. This story is also found in *Rawd Al-Unuf* by Imam As-Suhaili, Vol. III, pp. 267-271 and in books by Al-Tabari, Ibn Kathir, Ibn Khaldoon, Al-Booti, Al-Khudri and Al-Adid. All of these authors recite this gory story.

killing and torturing he carried out against their ancestors of the Banu Quraiza. The terrorism of our days did not come from nothing! Muslims – and the bloodbaths they are fond of – surely came from the deeds and acts of their example and prophet, and his successors and companions after him.

The acts of terrorism of that prophet were too many to be discussed in this book, and I cannot record all of his documented acts, but perhaps enough to cause a man's forehead to sweat with shame.

The Example of Fatima bint Rabi'a

Fatima bint Rabi'a was a woman who was used for an example because of her great honor and esteem. She refused to acknowledge Muhammad as a prophet. One time she cursed him, and Muhammad, the prophet of forgiveness, never forgot her. When Muhammad invaded the tribe of Banu Fazara, he killed most of its people but took Fatima bint Rabi'a, captive with her daughter.

Muhammad ordered that Fatima be tortured, as Al-Athir recorded in his book,[131] by commanding one of the deformed slaves to rape her daughter in front of her. After the slave finished his shameful act, Muhammad called upon Zayd bin Haritha and ordered him to kill Fatima, even though many people pleaded for clemency for her. Al-Tabari recorded:

"Muhammad ordered Zayd bin Haritha to kill Fatima, who was known as Umm Qirfa. He killed her violently by tying each of her feet by two ropes that were tied on two camels. He forced the camels to gallop in opposite directions and she was split into two halves."[132]

---

131) See *The Perfect in History* by Al-Athir, Vol. II, p. 142.
132) *The History of Nations and Kings* by Al-Tabari, Vol. II, p. 127.

She was a lady in her seventies, and she was split into two halves for merely cursing Muhammad. How disgusting! Could the god of Muhammad have inspired him to do that, as Muhammad himself claimed when some of his companion criticized him? How could Allah be so cruel when he is "the merciful, forgiving god?" It is inconceivable that there is a God who would order such terror. How far this is from Jesus Christ, who forgave those who crucified Him and even asked the Father to forgive those who killed him!

More about Safiya bint Huyay[133]

The story you just read was no different from the story of Kinana bin Al-Rabi'a, who was taken captive at the raid of Khaybar. Muhammad asked him the whereabouts of his fortune. In response, Kinana gave him all his wealth. Then Muhammad commanded that Kinana's wife be brought to watch, while he gave orders to Al-Zubeir bin Al-Awam to tie up Kinana. After taking off his clothes, they began to brand him with a branding iron in many sensitive areas of his body. Muhammad was sitting down, watching, with Kinana's wife, Safiya, sitting in his lap, forced to watch her husband being tortured. After the torture, Muhammad ordered him beheaded with the sword publicly, then he married his wife.

If any other prophet did what Muhammad did, Muslims would have said, "What kind of a prophet is that? What kind of butcher was he? What a Hitler!" They would have called him an animal, not a human – and definitely not a prophet. Please try to imagine this beastly cruelty, which surpassed all cruelties. Could that be the conduct of a prophet? O, sons of Islam, wake up!

---

133) See Chapter 2 for the basic story of Safiya, with documentation.

Permission from Allah

Some of the Muslims wanted to defect from Muhammad's religion because of the atrocities he committed. Many people became certain that Muhammad's claim to be a prophet could not be true. In fact, more than three thousand men defected from Islam after the raid of Kureiza, known by Muslims as the Battle of Al-Khandaq.[134]

As usual, Muhammad's solution was ready. Allah answered and "Gabriel" carried down all the necessary verses. Suddenly, Qur'anic verses came down upon him:

> "And he made you heirs of their lands, their houses, and their goods ... and Allah has power over all things."[135]

Muhammad claimed that his god approved of that. Could that really be God? Muhammad's god ordered him to loot, rob, kill, inherit people's lands and rape women publicly (as in the case of Fatima's daughter). Later, Allah ordered him to kill Kinana bin Rabi'a after torturing him and branding him with hot iron. In the story of Fatima, he tied her to two camels to split her in two parts. Muhammad's god ordered him to do all that? Those verses from Allah in the Qur'an (the Sura of Al-Ahzab) are very clear. What kind of god orders something so cruel, and allows killing, raping, adultery, robbing, and slavery? Surely that "god" was the fabrication of Muhammad's imagination. It could not be the real loving, merciful God.

The Raid of Al-Harkat

After the raid of Kurieza, where he killed over nine hundred men, looted their wealth and took their women as captives, he assaulted Al-Harkat, a Jewish village close to

134) That is, "Battle of the Trench," mentioned earlier this chapter.
135) Sura *Al-Ahzab* (the Allies) 33:9-27.

Medina, simply because he was not satisfied with destroying Kureiza. It is important to know that all the inhabitants of that village were killed. Muhammad bin Abd Al-Wahab wrote:

> "They (the Muslims) said, Allah is great, and they attacked as one soul, then they surrounded them and killed them by the swords of Allah."[136]

Muhammad made Allah carry the sword to kill the innocent. The Muslims fought in his name, but he is totally innocent of their claims? How could Allah kill his children without giving them a chance? How could Allah kill some innocent people that Muhammad took by surprise, without any crime being committed? Their only crime was that they were Jews who had some relations with Khaybar. He exercised vengeance against people who did nothing against him, killing everybody – men, women and children. Nothing remained except their wealth, which Muhammad gathered and took away, leaving behind a river of blood flowing through that village. After that, Muhammad prepared for his great invasion.

Muhammad's Ambition

Muhammad's raids were centered around Quraish and against the Jews of Khaybar, Atfan, Harfat and others. But the ambition of Muhammad and his companions expanded beyond the Arabian Peninsula to Byzantium. Muhammad sent one of his men[137] to Sharhabil bin Umar Al-Ghassani,[138] the Byzantine king, to present Muhammad's offers and demands. The king rejected the envoy and was of a mind to

---

136) *The Life of the Messenger*, by Muhammad bin Abd Al-Wahab, p. 111.
137) *One of his men*, that is, al Harith Ibn 'Umayr.
138) The *Al-Ghassanids* were an Arabic religious dynasty in southern Syria related to Catholicism, and an ally to the Byzantine empire.

march into Arabia, but changed his mind because Arabia was not worth the march. He figured it was an unpopulated desert inhabited only by some Bedouins with no natural resources.

Muhammad sent three leaders and a three-thousand-man army to invade Damascus. Unfortunately for them, they met the Byzantine army in the territory of the Jordan called Mu'tah. During the first battle[139], Zayd Ibn Haritha[140] was killed. He was replaced by Ja'far Ibn Abu Talib, who also was killed. After him, 'Abd Allah ibn Rawaha took over the leadership, but he was also killed and replaced by Khalid bin Al-Walid, who ordered his army to flee during the battle. The Arab army ran away during the night and returned to Medina, having lost more than 1,500 men.

In that battle, the god of Muhammad could not give him any victory. Some of those who were badly wounded, including 'Uthman bin Al-Maghira, asked Muhammad as soon as they returned: "Didn't the angels fight for us, O Messenger of Allah?" He answered: "Unfortunately, they were all busy someplace else." Thus, the god of Muhammad was too busy to help him, and "Gabriel" was on vacation. Could there be anything more absurd? How could people be convinced by such trickery and fraud?

Muhammad's deception succeeded because of the ignorance of Arabs in the age of ignorance. But how could Muhammad's deceiving words be accepted by well-educated people in the 21st century, an age of education, where science is providing many facts and awareness? Are Muslims unable to analyze and discern their own history?

History is full of stories of intimidation and terrorism

---

139) The Battle of Mu'tah was fought in 627.
140) *Zayd Ibn Haritha*, the adopted son of Muhammad. See Chapter 2.

in the days of Muhammad and after, under the banner of Islam, even to our present day. I would like to quote some of the records written by Muslim scholars, records of great shame that Muslims should find impossible to endure.

The Raid of the Christian 'Ukl tribe

There was an Arabian tribe called 'Ukl or 'Uraina that lived in peace and contentment. The people were all Christians. Muhammad raided them and turned their peace into a river of blood and tears. He ravaged the tribe, killing many men, and taking the rest as captives. Muhammad had the spoils carried back to Medina with him. A few hours after his arrival in Medina, the captives were brought into his presence. He asked them, "Is there someone to redeem you and pay your ransom?" They answered, "You took everything, and we have nothing left to give you." At that point, Ali bin Abu Talib demanded they curse Christ, but they would not. He then ordered them tortured then executed. About that shameful raid, Muslim scholar, Al-Khudri said:

> "A group of Arabian men came and killed one of Muhammad's companions. Consequently, Muhammad sent one hundred twenty horse riders who arrested them and brought them back to Muhammad who ordered them tortured while they were alive. Hands and legs were cut off, and eyes were nailed (meaning their eyes were pierced with hot nails). Then they were thrown in a ditch and were watched until they died.[141]

Sheikh Al-Khudri attempted to justify Muhammad's actions by accusing that tribe of killing one of his companions. However, those people did not kill anyone, and the assault

---

141) *The Light of Certainty* (Nur Al-Yaqin) by Al-Khudri, 24th edition, pp. 184-185.

was launched as all others, for robbing, raping and looting. Even if one of Muhammad's men was killed, would that justify the torturing and slaughtering of the whole tribe.

But Imam As-Suhaili, quoting Ibn Hisham, said:

> "After Muhammad arrested those men, he cut off their hands and their legs, and plucked out their eyes. They asked for water to drink, but Muhammad refused to give to them, until they died."[142]

That story was confirmed by Al-Bukhari in his Sahih.[143] Many Islamic references quoted the number of captives as forty-two. These were forty-two men, whose arms and legs were cut off and eyes were plucked out with hot nails, were then thrown in a ditch to die. Muhammad even refused to give them any water to drink. God help us.

Muslims say that Muhammad was the Seal of all God's Messengers and the prophet of mercy. *What* mercy? *What* peace? Could a natural person commit such outrageous crimes? Even a butcher and cutthroat would hesitate to do such atrocities as those Muhammad ordered and watched.

Some Muslims may say such accusations are false claims again their prophet Muhammad. I answer this: *I wish from the depth of my heart that this was a false claim, but the truth is always bitter.* I know this from experience because I felt the bitterness of the deeds of the prophet of Islam and the god of Islam as I discovered them for myself. It is dreadful, *very* dreadful, to attribute to the Holy, Pure God such false,

---

142) *Rawd Al-Unuf* by Imam As-Suhaili, Vol. III, p. 187.
143) See the *Hadith* of Sahih Bukhari, Vol. 1, Book 4, #234; Vol. 2, Book 24, #577; Vol. 4, Book 52, #261; Vol. 5, Book 59, #505; Vol. 6, Book 60, #134; Vol. 7, Book 71, #590 & 623; Vol. 8, Book 82, #794, 796, 797; and Vol. 9, Book 83, #37. See also the *Hadith* of Sahih Muslim, Book 16, #4130-37.

atrocities, when the real God is totally innocent of the claims
and deeds of Muhammad. The Creator of this universe could
never have any part in such horror and abomination.

Muhammad's Hobbies

Let us look at another story from Muslim books about
the life of Muhammad, "the master of the Messengers and
the Seal of all the prophets," as the Muslims believe.

Here is a prophet who was fond of bloodshed, whose
hobby was to have sex, and afterwards watch heads roll.
Here was a man who loved to see decapitated men's heads
brought to his presence. These included the head of his uncle Abu Al-Hakam[144], that was cut off by Ibn Mas'ood, the
heads of Sufyan bin Khalid and Ka'ab bin Ashraf, the two
Jews; also, the heads of Al-Qaisi, Asma' bint Marwan, Rifa'a
bin Qais, and Aqaba bin Abi Waqqas.[145]

A prophet and a messenger of Allah, Muhammad's first
hobby was having sex with younger women. His second
hobby was decapitating men and watching their execution.
His third hobby was torturing men, mutilating their bodies
while they were still alive, and then killing them. What a
prophet — who became an example to all Muslims! To top
it all off, Allah orders them:

> "So take what the Messenger assigns to you, and deny
> yourselves that which he withholds from you."[146]

"Follow Muhammad or Die"

When Amr bin Al-Aas arrived in Yemen to coerce its

---

144) *Abu Al-Hakam* – that is, the hated Abu-Jahl. See Chapter 3.
145) See *The Life of the Prophet* by Ibn Hisham, Vol. II, p. 146; *Al-Kamel
fi al-Tarikh (The Perfect in History)* by Ibn Al-Athir, Vol. II, p. 88; *The
Beginning and the End* by Ibn Kathir, Vol. II, p. 296; and *Al-Sira Al-
Halabia* by Al-Halabi, Vol. II, p. 12.
146) Sura *Hashr* (the Exile) 59:7, Yusuf Ali translation.

king to pay the tribute if he did not embrace Islam, the king asked him: "How did all Quraish become Muslims?" Al-Aas answered:

> "Quraish followed Muhammad either because they had the desire to embrace Islam, or because they were afraid as they were defeated by the sword. And now you are the only one left (who is not a Muslim). If you do not embrace Islam today, the horses will be treading all over you and your people. Embrace Islam and you will live in peace, and the horses and their riders will not attack you."

In other words, the choice was either Islam or death. Either follow Muhammad or die – a difficult choice and a most cruel terrorist tactic, fashioned by Muhammad the Messenger of Allah. Ibn Ishaq recorded:

> "The Messenger of Allah sent Khalid bin Al-Walid to bin Al-Harith, to the tribe of Najran, who were Christians, saying to him: If you embrace Islam and pay the alms, you will be accepted; but if you say no, I will kill you by the sword."[147]

The tribe sent some of the men of Al-Harith to the Messenger of Allah in obedience. What did the Messenger of Allah say to those fearful creatures?

> "Had you not embraced Islam, I would have rolled your heads under your feet!"[148]

Terror and terrorism was not demonstrated only in the deeds of Muhammad, but they were recorded as the revelation of his Allah in the Qur'an, inciting him to terrorize, kill and spill innocent blood. The Qur'an says:

147) *The Life of the Prophet*, Vol. IV, p. 134.
148) See *The Beginning and the End* by Ibn Kathir, Vol. V, p. 989; and *The Life of Muhammad* by Dr. Haikal, p. 488.

"And why should ye not kill in the cause of Allah, and .those who being weak, are ill-treated, men, women and children; whose cry is: Our Lord rescue us from this town, and raise for us from thee one who will protect us…"[149]

Verse 74 of the same Sura says:

"Let those fight in the cause of Allah, who sell the life of this world for the hereafter, to him who fighteth in the cause of Allah, whether he is slain or gets victory —soon shall We give him a reward of great (value)."[150]

The Sura of Muhammad says:

"Therefore, when you meet the unbelievers, smite at their necks … when you have thoroughly subdued them, bind a bond firmly (on them), thereafter (is the time for) either generosity or ransom: until the war lays down its burdens."[151]

Sura *Al-Ma'idah* says:

"…And fight in his cause that you may prosper."[152]

Sura *Al-Anfal* says:

"Against them make ready your strength to the utmost of your power, including steeds of war, to strike terror into (the hearts of) the enemies … and others besides, whom ye may not know, but whom Allah doth know …."[153]

---

149) Sura *An-Nisa'* (the Women) 4:75, author's translation.

150) More Qur'an verses that provoke Muslims to fight and incite them to kill include Sura *An-Nisa'* (the Women) 4:76, 77, 89, 91, 95 & 104.

151) Sura *Muhammad* 47:4, Yusuf Ali translation.

152) Sura *Al-Ma'idah* (the Table) 5:35, author's translation.

153) Sura *Al-Anfal* (the Spoils of War) 8:60, Yusuf Ali translation.

Love vs. Terror

Terror here is clearly commanded, and he urged Muslims to strike terror in the heart of the enemy. Islam rose to take terror, terrorism and terrorizing as a means of convincing people to embrace a religion that was clearly of Muhammad's own making, with no heavenly foundations.

Heaven does not carry the sword, nor does it command the spilling of innocent blood. Heaven declares: "Love your enemy." It does not say, "Butcher your enemies." Heaven says: "Bless them who curse you."

It is not possible for Heaven to say:

> "O Messenger, rouse the Believers to the fight. If there are twenty amongst you, patient and persevering, they will vanquish two hundred: if a hundred, they will vanquish a thousand of the Unbelievers: for these are a people without understanding."[154]

Heaven says,

> "...whosoever shall smite thee on thy right cheek, turn to him the other also." [155]

But Heaven would not say that God will fight for Muslims, as the Sura of Muhammad tried to project:

> "Be not weary and faint-hearted, crying for peace, when ye should be the uppermost; for Allah is with you, and will never put you in loss for your (good) deeds."[156]

God, the master of heaven, and the Creator of earth, life and this whole universe, would not incite people to kill and commit aggression. What god would order people to kill

---

154) Sura *Al-Anfal* (the Spoils of War) 8:65, Yusuf Ali translation.
155) Matthew 5:39.
156) Sura *Muhammad* 47:35, Yusuf Ali translation.

Jews and Christians, when they are referred to in the Qur'an as the people of the Book?[157] What kind of a god orders Christians, and those who back them, killed and dispersed, as the Qur'an states:

"If ye gain the mastery over them in war, disperse them, and those who are backing them, that they remember."[158]

For those who would like to read more about killing and fighting in the Qur'an, there are numerous examples. These verses, which fill the Qur'an, incite Muslim to fight, scatter, torture and butcher all who disobey Muhammad or refuse to embrace Islam, or Muslims who abandon Islam.[159]

The killing sword was not limited to the unbeliever, but had its frightening effects on Muslims themselves as they began to kill each other after the coming down of the Qur'an, as will be discussed later. We will view how Muslims proved to be traders of prestigious positions for which they have been ready to fight and kill even each other.

All Islamic conquests after Muhammad were accomplished by the edge of the sword. Ibn Al-Asam Al-Garhami said in his book *Tales of Battles* that the number killed from the beginning of Muhammad's calling until his death was over 30,000 men. And those who met their doom by the Islamic sword from the beginning of the Islamic call until 1250 Hijra (equivalent to about 1750 AD) was about ten million people. In Spain alone, Muslims killed over one and

---

157) *People of the Book*, that is, people of the Bible.
158) Sura *Al-Anfal* (the Spoils of War) 8:57, author's translation.
159) See *An-Nisa'* (the Women) 4:71, 74-77, 88-89, 91, 95, and 104; Sura *Al-Ma'idah* (the Table) 5:35, 45 & 51; Sura *Al-Anfal* (the Spoils of War) 8:12-13, 16-17, 19, 36, 39, 45, 60, and 65; Sura *At-Tauba* (Repentance) 9:81, 83, 86, 111, and 123; Sura *Muhammad* 47:4, 20, 31, and 35; and Sura of *Al-Fath* (Victory) 48:25.

a half million men from the eighth century until they were forced out of Spain in 1492.

Al-Riddah: War of the Backsliders

What about Muslims killing Muslims? From Muhammad's death until 1990, over ten million Muslims have been killed, mostly in attempts to usurp government authority. When Muhammad was still alive, many of his followers became certain that his religion was man-made and not from God. As a result, tens of thousands of his followers backslid from Islam. Abu Bakr, the first Caliph (successor) demanded that they should pay the alms[160] required of Muslims. When they refused, he made his famous statement:

> "I swear by Allah, if they ceased to pay me what they used to pay the Messenger of Allah, I will fight them."

However, Umar Ibn al-Khattab objected to the decision of Abu Bakr at the beginning and said to him:

> "Abu Bakr, how will you fight people about whom the Prophet said, I was ordered to fight people until they say: No god but Allah, and that Muhammad is the Messenger of Allah?"

Abu Bakr, who was taught by Muhammad to rob people's wealth, disperse them, then take them captive and kill them, answered: "But they refuse to pay the Alms!" As a result, the war against the backsliders began, not for refusing to confess that there is no god but Allah, but because they did not pay the Alms to Abu Bakr as they did to Muhammad.

In the vicious War of the Backsliders (Al-Riddah),[161] Abu

---

160) *Alms* – that is, *Al-Zakat*, 2.5% of one's wealth, collected to give to the poor and needy. This is one of the 5 pillars of Islam.
161) *Al-Riddah* was fought for 2 years after Muhammad's death (632).

Bakr killed over thirty thousand men who rejected Muhammad and refused to pay the required Alms.

You remember the story of Aisha and Safwan[162] and her grudge against Ali, who advised Muhammad to apply to her the rule of Islam on adultery. The Prophet rescued her from Ali's sword with a verse that came down by "Gabriel," vindicating her of adultery. Aisha never forgot what Ali said to Muhammad against her. As a result, she formed an alliance with Mu'awiyah against Ali. She led a three-day battle against him in the city of Basra in Iraq in the year 34 Hijra. The battle was called the Battle of the Camel[163] because Aisha was in the midst of the battle on a camel.

During that battle, more than ten thousand Muslims were killed on both sides. After the funerals that were officiated by Ali and Aisha, Aisha was asked:

> "O Mother of the Believers, which of those will go to paradise?"

Aisha pretended to have forgotten what her husband, the prophet, had said:

> "If two Muslims fought against each other with their swords, the killer and the killed will go to the fire of hell."

So she answered:

> "All of them are going to paradise."[164]

Of course, the only "paradise" they went to was in the

---

162) See Chapter 4.

163) The first major Muslim civil war, fought at Basra, Iraq in 656. Also known as the "Battle of Bassora" or "Battle of Jamal."

164) See the *Hadith* of Sahih Bukhari Vol. 1, Book 2, #30; Vol. 9, Book 83, #14; Vol. 9, Book 88, #204; and the *Hadith* of Sahih Muslim Book 41, Chapter 4, "When Two Muslims Confront Each Other with Swords," #6898-6901.

imaginative minds of Muslims, drawn and adorned by Muhammad!

War between Muslims:
The Assassination of 'Uthman ibn 'Affan

The most dangerous and important incidences were the assassinations of the successors of Muhammad (called the Caliphs) and Muslim leaders. One of those was 'Uthman ibn 'Affan, the third Caliph, who donated 10,000 dinars to Muhammad when he first began to propagate his calling. Al-Halabi wrote about him:

> "'Uthman ibn 'Affan came with ten thousand dinars cash and placed them in the hands of Muhammad and in his bosom. Muhammad began to grab the money, examine it, turning it every which direction, carefully and joyfully, saying, 'May Allah give you his forgiveness on all your sins, the secret ones and the public ones, O 'Uthman. May Allah give you forgiveness for what you did in the past and what you will do in the future unto the day of resurrection. Nothing 'Uthman will do will hurt him from this day on.'"[165]

Islamic writers[166] give us more details of his assassination. Two influential Muslim men, Muhammad bin Abu Bakr and Ammar bin Yasir, entered into the presence of 'Uthman while he was reading the Qur'an of Muhammad. They tortured him, then killed him. They also stepped on his beard with their shoes – a sign of great insult. (Don't forget that

---

165) *Al-Sira Al-Halabia* by Al-Halabi, Vol. III, p. 100. See also *The Jurisprudence of the Life of Muhammad* by Al-Bouti, p. 309; *The Beginning and the End* by Ibn Kathir, Vol. V, p. 4; and *Asad Al Ghaba (The Lion of the Forest)* by Ibn Al-Athir, Vol. III, p. 588.

166) See Footnote #59 above for the documentation.

'Uthman was one of the ten carriers of the good tidings who preached about Paradise. He was the one to whom Muhammad had given assurances that all his sins, past and future, were forgiven, after he paid the ten thousand dinars.)

The irony was that he was killed by another carrier of the good tidings about Paradise, Ammar bin Yasir, who came from a clan who were tortured by the Quraish for Muhammad. But all Muhammad could do was to say,

> "Be patient Sarafan (the leader of the clan), for the promise of Paradise is yours; and both of them were great Muslims."

Remember, Muhammad said that the killer and the killed both go to the fire of hell. Did 'Uthman really go to Paradise because of the ten thousand dinars that he donated to Muhammad, and for which he was promised Paradise? Did Ammar bin Yasir, one of the carriers of the good tidings about Paradise, who killed a fellow Muslim, go to Paradise? Are Muslims thinking about these things? Are 'Uthman and Ammar going to heaven or to hell? According to Muhammad, they were going to heaven. But also according to Muhammad they were going to hell.

'Uthman was the husband of two of Muhammad's daughters, Ruqayyah and Umm Kulthum. Muhammad said of him: "If I had forty daughters, I would have married them to 'Uthman." However, this third Caliph was killed by Ammar and the son of the first Caliph.

The Battle of Siffin[167]

Over fifteen thousand Muslim men were killed during the Battle of Siffin, where Ali bin Abu Talib fought against Mu'awiyah Ibn Abi-Sufyan (The leader of the Umayyads,

---

167) Fought May-July 657 in Syria, by the Euphrates River.

who started the Umayyad Empire). This conflict was over the succession to the Caliphate, after the assassination of 'Uthman. Did those men go to hell or Paradise?

The Battle of Karbala[168]

A few years after that vicious battle, Ali's sons, Al-Hassan and Al-Hussein, met the son of Mu'awiyah in another vicious battle, in the city of Karbala, Iraq, where over fifteen thousand Muslims were killed and Al-Hussein bin Ali was beheaded. His corpse was grotesquely disfigured, and his head was hanged on a pole publicly. His wife and all his children (the grandsons and the great-grandsons of Muhammad) were killed.

The Battle of the Zab[169]

Many years later, the Abbasids staged a coup and took the authority from the Umayyads. (They were called Abbasids after Abbas, Muhammad's uncle.) They did not forget what the Umayyads did to the grandchildren of Muhammad and their families, so they decided to avenge their deaths. The Abbasid prince, Abu Al-Abbas, who was given the name, the butcher, completely annihilated the descendents of the Umayyads, including the women, the teenagers, and the infants. Even their graves were not safe, for they were dug up, the corpses defiled, and some parts were given to stray dogs. Wow! What kind of religion is this Islam?

The Battle of Ain Jalut[170]

The history of Islam is shameful by all measures. Under its own banner Muslims robbed, looted, and executed their innocent captives and disfigured the corpses of the dead.

168) Fought October 10, 680. Karbala is 60 miles SW of Baghdad.
169) Fought January 25, 750 by the Great Zab river in Iraq.
170) *Ain Jalut* (Eye [or Spring] of Goliath), fought September 3, 1260 in Palestine.

They also tortured their captives before killing them, from the days of Muhammad until our very days. What they did in Spain, Portugal, Chad, and some Asian countries surpasses all imagination and description. Many Muslim scholars believed the Tartars[171] and their leader, Holako, were Muslims. In their march, they looted, butchered, and burnt many Muslim and non-Muslim cities, until they were defeated by Qutuz the Sultan of Egypt in the Battle of Ain Jalut.

The Ottoman Massacres

However, the Ottoman Turks were famous for their cruel governmental control that resulted in atrocious massacres launched indiscriminately against many nations in Europe, the Middle East, and North Africa. The Ottoman Sultans were known as cruel rulers who killed anyone who disobeyed them or hesitated to pay the Alms (tribute) to the High Gate, the Sultan's palace in Istanbul. For four hundred years, they conducted many massacres in every country they colonized. The massacres against the Armenians in 1917 resulted in the murder of over one million unarmed men.

Iraq vs. Iran

In this age of knowledge and science, we ask, "What are Muslims doing to themselves? For example, the Iraqis fought against the Iranians for eight years, resulting in the death of more than one million Iraqis, and one and one half million Iranians, plus more than six million men wounded, and thousands of disabled.

Iraq vs. Kuwait

After that, the Iraqis invaded Kuwait under the direction of the Butcher, Saddam Hussein, who killed thousands of people, robbed, stole and dispersed the Kuwaitis through-

---

171) In modern literature called "Tatars."

out the world, until they restored their land with the help of mainly Christian Americans and Europeans. Notice, it was mainly Christians who restored Kuwait to the Kuwaitis. Kuwaitis are Muslims, but it was largely Christians who restored them to their land and are protecting them from an invasion by someone who claims to be a grandchild of Muhammad. I do not doubt Hussein's claim because his deeds mirrored and are no less evil than those of Muhammad.

Yemen and Afghanistan

Then the Yemenis massacred each other in 1994 in a war between North and South Yemen, where more than 10,000 men were slaughtered. However, in Afghanistan, the Afghanis fought against the Russians to gain their independence and won. But then they turned against each other and fought for about twenty years. That war resulted in more than one million dead Afghanis. The Taliban won the struggle and took over the government. But they were not satisfied by becoming the rulers of Afghanistan; they decided to export their terror to the rest of the world. Even Muslim countries were not safe from their terror.

Exporting Terrorism

Men from Egypt, Algeria, Saudi Arabia, Yemen and other Muslim countries left their homelands to help the Afghani people gain their independence from the Soviets. But what was the result of the help they received from those Arabs who came from the other Arab countries? In the end, those Arab fighters settled in Afghanistan. (By the way, the horrendous destruction they caused was not against the Soviets, who finally withdrew from Afghanistan, but against Afghanistan itself – its people, its buildings, its roads and its land.)

Those terrorists who settled in Afghanistan decided to

export terrorism to their own native countries. Egypt suffered much, as Egyptians and tourists were targeted; but the main targets there were the Egyptian Christian Coptics, who constituted 80% of all the victims in Egypt.

As a result of the export of terrorism from Afghanistan, Algeria, Saudi Arabia, Sudan and other Arab countries paid an exorbitant price. But that terror was not confined to the Arab world, for it spread throughout Europe, the United States of America, as well as Asian countries.

Muhammad, the prophet of Islam, and their example, said in a Hadith, recorded in the *Hadith* of Sahih Bukhari:

> "Fight the unbelievers (Christians and Jews), until they declare, 'No god but Allah, and Muhammad is the Messenger of Allah.' And if they did not say it, their captives are your bond-slaves, and their wealth are yours. Their women and children are lawfully yours."[172]

This is what Muhammad, the Prophet of Allah, the Seal of the prophets, said to his followers. Oh, Muslims of the earth, you have ignored the truth long enough, and the saying of Salah Jahine:[173]

> "O for a nation that can not see even though its eyes are open."

---

172) This is the meaning behind the *Hadith* of Sahih Bukhari, Vol. 1, Book 2, # 24; Vol. 1, Book 8, #387; and the *Hadith* of Sahih Muslim, Book 31, #5917. Other partial quotes can be found in the *Hadith* of Sahih Bukhari Vol. 2, Book 23, #483; Vol. 9, Book 84, #59; Vol. 9, Book 88, #215-216; Vol. 9, Book 92, #388; and the *Hadith* of Sahih Muslim, Book 1, #29-35; Book 19, #4294. These and other *ahadith* interpret the meaning of an oft-used statement by Muhammad from the Qur'an, Sura *Al-Baqara* (the Cow) 2:193.

173) *Salah Jahine* (1930-1986) was an Egyptian poet.

Libya vs. Chad

Then came Mu'ammar al-Qadhafi of Libya, a revolutionary colonel, who did not finish high school. Yet he authored the green book, wherein he contradicted the Qur'an, described Muhammad in strange ways and accused Muslim pilgrims to Mecca of being heathens. He was a Muslim colonel who attacked the Muslims and Christians of Chad, Central Africa and killed about ten thousand people in Ugenka, and the valley of Aozou, in Chad. The scars of his actions and the results of the slaughter he conducted in Chad are still showing. Another result of the teaching of Muhammad!

These hateful actions have not been just coincidences, but rather are the real results of Muhammad's education of his people. He began his calling with raiding, spilling blood and killing. After he gained greater influence, he developed a killing machine with his victims numbering in the thousands. And the number of people made homeless by him and his companions after him was in the hundreds of thousands. You cannot see one single Islamic government, from the beginning of Islam until now, that was not stained with much innocent blood.

Saudi Arabia

Saudi Arabia tops the list of the countries that embrace Islam, both constitutionally and judicially. Saudi children study the life of Muhammad and the Qur'an and memorize much, if not all, of it. Consequently, they are the people who are most inclined to use the cowards' means of terrorism. For example, bin Laden is a Saudi who was born in Saudi Arabia and studied the Qur'an there. He has become a household name because of his terrorism. He tops the Most Wanted list worldwide. When you look at the list of terrorists who destroyed the World Trade Center towers, you find that fifteen of the nineteen terrorists were Saudis. That's what Muhammad taught them. They were following the instructions of Muhammad, to destroy and to kill the innocent, including men, women and children.

Sudan and Beyond

During the 1990s, more that thirty-four wars raged in the world. It is amazing to know that thirty-two of those wars were *Islamic* wars. In Sudan, the Muslim authorities decided to Islamize all the citizens by brutal force, if needed. When the southern Sudan rejected Islam, a vicious war was declared. Homes, villages and towns were destroyed. Hundreds of thousands of people were killed. Christian women and children were taken captive and sold in slave markets for years. We are talking about the public selling of humans at the end of the 20th century and the beginning of the 21st!

Even as I write, Sudanese are terrorizing their Christian population. There is neither time nor space in this book to write about Islamic atrocities taking place in the Philippines, Algeria, Iraq, Iran, Yemen, Afghanistan, Syria, Bosnia, Pakistan, Indonesia, India, Syria, Egypt, Cyprus, Monte Negro, Lebanon, Nigeria, Azerbaijan, and others.

What kind of god did Muhammad serve? It is impossible to believe that the True God would encourage His followers to kill, destroy, rob and spill the blood of the innocent. It becomes obvious that his god was not the true God. Muhammad's god was hand-made for his own purposes. Yes, there was an "angel" for Muhammad, whose name was unfortunately stolen from the Bible. And upon that angel Muhammad dumped much suffering and tragedy, by attributing to him all those verses that justified the atrocities Muhammad inflicted. Yes, Muhammad was very intelligent devise such a god and such an angel, but his intelligence was satanic.

In the next chapter I will reveal many of the mistakes that fill the pages of the Qur'an: grammatical, historical, archeological and scientific. Also, I will reveal contradictions in the Qur'an to show that it cannot be from the True God who is *really* the "All-knowing."

Then I will discuss a very important subject that Muslim scholars call "The Annulling and the Annulled." This is where Allah sends a verse, then, as though apologizing for his mistake of sending it, sends *another* verse to correct his own mistake, "annulling" the previous verse. Those annulling verses sometimes came down only a few hours after the "wrong" verses came upon Muhammad.

Then we will answer an even bigger question: "Was the Qur'an sent from God or made-up by man?"

5

Is the Qur'an
God-Sent or Man-Made?

Mr. Qasem, my old teacher of Religion, stated (as all Muslim Imams and Sheikhs say) that the miracle that Muhammad performed was the writing of the Qur'an. They claim that the Qur'an is the most eloquent, best piece of rhetoric ever written, because it is a heavenly book and not man-made. The Qur'an itself includes in its text a challenge to any man to produce a like-Qur'an or even a like-verse. Dr. Badawi, a religion teacher in high school, said "The Qur'an is the last heavenly book and Muhammad is the last prophet and the seal thereof."

Could those statements be true? In this chapter, we will investigate "the eloquence of the Qur'an" to see if it *is* "the most eloquent" and "a miracle." Then we will answer the question of whether the Qur'an is heavenly or man-made.

Until recently, despite my doubts, I had a good amount of faith in the above subject. I used to defend the Qur'an, and I was a fan of Sheikh Abdul Baset[174] who chanted the

174) Abdul Baset Abdel Samad, a popular reciter of the Qur'an.

114

Qur'an, and whose voice I enjoyed very much. I believed, as all Muslims believe, that the Qur'an is a heavenly book, and that Islam, in general, was the seal of all religion, and that it came down from God. Then some whispering voice came to me and warned me: "Read in depth. Read and reflect upon the verses and upon what is in between the lines." I began to read, indeed, and what have I found?

Qur'anic Copying

As I reflected on the Qur'an, I also reflected on the Bible, which I also read. I learned that many verses in the Qur'an are taken from the Bible, with some additions and changes.

For example, the Qur'an imposed on every Muslim the obligation to pay 2.5% for alms.[175] That copies the Old Testament, which ordained for the Jews to pay 10% of their yearly income. The Qur'an also designated specific times during the day for prayer. The Bible commands us to pray, but it does not designate a time. The Bible gives the right to pray any time and anywhere.

Fasting in the Qur'an is also copied from the Bible, with some modifications. Most of the general imperatives in the Qur'an were copied from the Bible, with either additions or subtractions. One Bible verse copied by the Qur'an is:

"The fear of God is the beginning of wisdom."[176]

It appeared that Muhammad's "Gabriel" was dipping into the Bible with some modifications on the verses.

The Qur'an on Muhammad

Verses about the personal life of Muhammad were stated in the Qur'an to permit certain things in Muhammad's life

---

175) *2.5%* - that is, *Al-Zakat*. See Chapter 4, Footnote #54.
176) The Bible, Job 28:28; Psalm 111:10; Proverbs 9:10; & Ecclesiastes 12:13. The Qur'anic copy is found at Sura *Al-Fatir* (the Creator) 35:28.

while prohibiting them from the daily life of the rest of the Muslims. For example, his marriages, his divorces, and his distribution of spoils all had their verses.

Distorted History

Muslims describe the Qur'an as telling the history of the world. But what little historical facts appear in the Qur'an, whether religious or mundane, are distorted quotes from the Bible. The Qur'an did not come up with anything new; it just changed the story for an Arabic audience.

For instance, the Qur'an tells the stories of Joseph, Job, Moses, Aaron (Moses' brother), their dealing with Pharaoh, and crossing the Red Sea to Sinai and to the Jordan. I wish he had quoted those stories as they are in the Bible. Instead they were rewritten in his Qur'an, adding information and fabricating events that never happened. These will be discussed later. It is important to know that most Qur'anic verses are centered on daily happenings during Muhammad's life. Therefore, most verses of the Qur'an are not applicable to all times and to every generation.

The Miracle of the Qur'an?

Now I will focus on what the Muslims call the "miraculousness" of the Qur'an. By this they mean it does not contain any mistake, whether grammatical, historical or biblical, and no human can come close to writing anything like it. I, till recently, challenged followers of other religions to find one single mistake in our beloved Qur'an. But some dear friends told me to read it carefully and thoroughly to find out for myself. I did, and I was shocked to find innumerable grammatical and historical errors.

[Note: Following are a few of the many *mistakes* in the Arabic grammar of the Qur'an. They are shown in Arabic, so those who know Arabic can see the obvious errors.]

Male vs. Female, Singular vs. Plural, Subject vs. Object

In Sura *Al-A'raf* below,[177] Muhammad referred to the number in the female form, when the correct form would be the male form. Then he wrote the word in the plural that was supposed to be in the singular.

(كتب : "وقطعناهم اثنتي عشرة أسباطا.» (الأعراف 160

«وكان بنبغي أن يكتب : «وقطعناهم اثني عشر سبطاً».

In the next verse, from Sura *At-Tauba*,[178] he wrote in the singular form what should have been written in the plural form:

(كتب : "وخضتم كالذي خاضوا.» (التوبة ١٩

«وكان ينبغي أن يكتب: «وخضتم كالذين خاضوا».

Muhammad also managed to put the subject form in place of the object form and vice-versa – an unforgivable mistake in the Arabic language, as in Sura *Al-Hajj*:[179]

(كتب : "هذان خصمان اختصوا في ربهم» (الحج 19

«وكان ينبغي أن يكتب : «هذان خصمان اختصما في ربهما».

Another verse with a gross mistake is in Sura *Ta Ha*:[180]

(كتب : "إن هذان لساحران.» (طه 63 .

«وكان ينبغي أن يكتب : «إن هذين لساحران».

Here is a gross error that would have made Muhammad flunk Arabic class, in Sura *Al-Ma'idah*[181]

(كتب : "إن الذين آمنوا والذين هادوا والصابئين.» (المائدة 69

«وكان ينبغي أن يقول : «إن الذين آمنوا والذين هادوا والصابئون».

---

177) See Sura *Al-A'raf* (the Heights), 7:160.
178) See Sura *At-Tauba* (Repentance) 9:69.
179) See Sura *Al-Hajj* (the Pilgrimage) 22:69
180) See Sura *Ta Ha* 20:63.
181) See Sura *Al-Ma'idah* (the Table) 5:69.

Another clear mistake, in Sura *Al-Baqara*:[182]

(كتب : "لا ينال عهدي الظالمين.» (البقرة ١٢٤

«.وكان ينبغي أن يقول : «لا ينال عهدي الظالمون

In Sura *Al-A'raf*:[183], the male form was written mistakenly for the female form (a huge grammatical mistake)...

(كتب : "إن رحمة الله قريب.» (الأعراف 56

«.وكان ينبغي أن يقول : «إن رحمة الله قريبة

Here, the form of the verb was changed from present tense to the imperative mood (a major error), in *Al-Munafiqun*:[184]

كتب : "ربي لولا اخرتني إلى اجل قريب فأصدق وأكن من الصالحين.»
((المنافقون ١٠

وكان ينبغي أن يقول : «ربي لولا اخرتني إلى اجل قريب فأصدق وأكون من
الصالحين.»

As mentioned before, numerous major grammatical mistakes fill the Qur'an. Muslim scholars are quite aware that pagan pieces of literature hung on the walls of the Ka'aba (المعلقات) were without any grammatical mistakes. They were much more eloquent rhetoric than the "miraculous" Qur'an, even though the authors were mere humans. True, they were well-known poets and writers, but they were not prophets or gods, just human beings make mistakes. *But they did not.*

Those pieces of literature were so astounding that Arab poets, and writers of the present and past centuries have not been able to match such eloquence.

In the meantime, the Qur'an, believed by Muslims to be miraculous, *is full of mistakes*. Should we say that those pagan Arabic writings (which are without mistakes) were miraculous? Al-Suyuti said:

---

182) See Sura *Al-Baqara* (the Cow) 2:124.
183) See Sura *Al-A'raf* (the Heights) 7:56.
184) See Sura *Al-Munafiqun* (the Hypocrites) 63:10

"It is not lawful, at all, to read the Qur'an without reading it in the Arabic language; even if the reader is not good at reading Arabic."

He said this because most Muslim scholars agree that translating the Qur'an into other languages causes it to lose much of its meaning and eloquence. They claim that when it was translated into English it lost its linguistic value.

If it is not lawful for people to read the Qur'an or pray in any language other than Arabic, we must ask:

"Is Allah the god of the Arabs only?" "Is he not the God of all people?" "Does He not speak other languages—or only the Arabic, as Muhammad mentioned several times in the Qur'an?"

Muhammad went even further, claiming that the language of heaven will be Arabic, even though there are less than three hundred million Arabic-speaking people in the world. The population of the world, as we enter the 21st century, is over six billion people. *That means only 5% speak Arabic.*

Muhammad said:

"Love the Arabs for three reasons: because I am an Arab, because the Qur'an came down upon us in Arabic,[185] and because the language of the people in Paradise is Arabic."[186]

---

185) More specifically, the Qur'an was "revealed" in the Quraish dialect. See the *Hadith* of Sahih Bukhari, Vol. 6, Book 61, #507.

186) See *Hadith* #5751 (Mishkat, Vol. 3). Not in the *Ahadith* of Bukhari or Muslim, but is a genuine saying of Muhammad, according to *Al-Qari's Dictionary of Hadith Forgeries (Al-Asrar Al-Marfu'a)*, translation and notes by GF Haddad. Arabic also emphasized in the Qur'an. See Suras *Ash-Shu'ara'* (the Poets) 26:195; *Az-Zumar* (the Crowds) 39:28; *Ha Mim Sajdah* (Revelations Well-Expounded) 41:3, 44; *Ash-Shura* (the Counsel) 42:7; *Az-Zukhruf* (the Embellishment) 43:3; *Ad-Dukhan* (the Smoke) 44:58; *Al-Ahqaf* (the Sandhills) 46:12; and *An-Nahl* (the Bee) 16:103.

However, the Arabian Prophet contradicted himself in another place, saying:

> "There is no difference between an Arab and a non-Arab except in piety."[187]

If the Qur'an was meant for the whole world, it should come in the language that could be translated without much loss in value and meaning. Moreover, if the Qur'an was from God, it should be applicable to every generation and every place, not just for Arabs, and only during a certain epoch!

Other Reasons for Confusion

When the Qur'an was written, it didn't have the needed dots on the letters,[188] which are most important in Arabic. The Sheikh of Islam, Ibn Taymiyyah,[189] wrote:

> "The companions of Muhammad did not put the dots on the letters nor did they put the accents on the letters. For this, the word could be read two different ways, having two different meanings such as:

ون و يعلمون   . .

صار وضار . ش س

This particular fact – the writing of the Qur'an without dots – was confirmed by Al-Suyuti.[190]

That there are many mistakes in the Qur'an is well known among Muslims, and cannot be denied by their scholars. I ask: "Did not "Gabriel" realize the importance of the accents and dots on letters when the Qur'an was sent down?"

---

187) See Chapter 3, Footnote #18 for details.
188) Called "diacritical points," which may change the actual meaning of a word or a word's tense, voice or mood; or they may distinguish between one word and a completely different word.
189) *Majmoo' Al-Fatawa* (Compilation of Fatawa), Vol. XVII, p. 101.
190) See *Al-Ittiqan* by Al-Suyuti, Vol. I, p. 160. See also *Behind the Veil: Unmasking Islam* by Abd El Schafi (1996), pp. 189-194.

Long after the Qur'an was written, Abu Al-Aswad Al-Du'ali and Saybubia (Khalil Ibn Ahmad) finished the job "Gabriel" was incapable of doing. When putting the accents and dots on the letters was finished, a clash happened among Muslims, and it is still going on today: the Qur'an is being read in two different ways, and Muslim scholars confirm that fact! However, Muhammad confessed that the Qur'an could be read in seven different ways (that would give different meanings to many of its words) as was recorded in the *Ahadith* of Al-Bukhari and Muslim.[191]

Differences in the recitation of the Qur'an by different Muslim scholars have caused many different interpretations of the laws and the legislation of different Muslim countries.[192]

When I was a young child, I asked my religion teacher why the alif was deleted from all the words where it should have been placed. He had no answer then, and Muslim scholars still do not have an answer. I wondered if "Gabriel," the archangel, had eaten that alif on his way down to dictate those words to Muhammad. Who knows? Maybe the dictionary of "Gabriel" did not have the alif in it.

They say the Qur'an is a miracle. Could it be a miracle because of the hundreds of *verses* that no one has been able to find a meaning for? It is even hard to find meanings for some of the *words*!

Once, an Arabian asked Abu Bakr about the phrase in

---

191) See the *Hadith* of Sahih Bukhari, Vol. 3, Book 41, #601; Vol. 4, Book 54, #442; Vol. 6, Book 61, #513-514; Vol. 9, Book 93, #640; and the *Hadith* of Sahih Muslim, Book 4, Chapter 139: "'The Qur'an Has Been Revealed in Seven Modes of Reading' and Its Meaning," #1782-1790.
192) For more information, see *Al-Ittiqan* by Al-Suyuti, Vol. 1, pp. 157 & 226, and other sections of Part Four in his book.

the Qur'an, "And the fruit and Abban وفاكهة وأبًا". He answered, "I cannot explain what I do not know." But Umar
Ibn Al-Khattab, the third Caliph, said sarcastically in one of
his Friday sermons:

> "The fruit we do know, but what is the meaning of
> Abban? I personally challenge the Muslim scholars
> to tell me the meaning of the phrase in Sura of Mary
> 19:13 where it says: 'وحنان من لدنا وزكوة وكان تقيا'."

(I wrote the above phrase in Arabic because it cannot be
understood or translated coherently). Muslim scholars gave
it twelve different interpretations. Sa'id Ibn Jubeir wrote
about this verse:

> "I asked Sa'id Ibn Abbas about it, but he did not
> answer me."

The Imam Al-Suyuti quoted Ibn Abbas himself:

> "I do not know the meaning of many words in the
> Qur'an."

I also want to note some words and letters that are sym-
bols in the Qur'an to see if anyone has an interpretation:

"خ م و ن و ك هـ ي ع ص ، ح م ع س ق ...إلخ"

Al-Suyuti wrote:

> "The beginning of all the suras are mysteries that no
> one knows the meaning thereof except for Allah."

When they asked him what TAH, YASEEN and SAD
طه ، ياسين وص mean, he said:

> "I do not know. However, I think TAHA and YAS-
> EEN were names that Muhammad's god used to
> call him by. For example, when his god addressed
> him in the sura, he said: 'TAHA, we have not sent
> down the Qur'an to thee to be in distress.' So was
> also the word YASEEN used. But I surely confess

that I am incapable of knowing the meaning of SSAD and QAF."[193]

The Qur'an itself acknowledges that it quotes Bible verses and stories. One admission is in the following verse:

"He is he who sent down upon you, and from him, commanding verses from the <u>very Book</u>, and others like them."[194] In this verse, the alif was deleted from three words represented in the highlighted ones.

Meaninglessness!

Many Qur'an verses have no meaning, and if a meaning is given, Muslim scholars differ with each other concerning it. For example, Sura *Ar-Rahman*, 55:6, says:

"The star and the tree both bow down in adoration."

On this, Al-Baydawi,[195] Jalalayn[196] and Zamkhashri[197] all agreed that "star" means some herbs. But many other scholars, especially the contemporaries, disagree, saying it means the stars in heaven. Even in different English translations of the Qur'an, some translations use the word herbs, and others use star. But there is no relation between stars and herbs.[198]

As mentioned above, there have always been clashes among Muslims on the interpretation of meaningless verses.[199]

The Qur'an is full of grammatical mistakes, historical mistakes and many meaningless phrases that no one can be sure

---

193) *Al-Ittiqan* by Al-Suyuti, Vol. III, p. 29.
194) Sura *Al-Imran* (the Family of Imran) 3:7, author's translation.
195) *Al-Baydawi*, p. 705.
196) *Jalalayn*, p. 450.
197) *Al-Kashaf* by Al-Zamkhashri, Vol. IV, p. 443.
198) For instance, compare Yusuf Ali's "herbs" to Pickthall's "stars!"
199) More meaningless verses can be found in: Suras *Al-Baqara* (the Cow) 2:143; *At-Tauba* (Repentance) 9:85; *Al-Qiyamah* (the Resurrection) 75:17; and *Al-Furqan* (the Criterion) 25:43.

what they mean, Yet Muslims still boast that the Qur'an is a linguistic Miracle. They even dare to challenge, and the Qur'an itself challenges, people to write at least one verse that matches its eloquence. Muhammad boasted that it was his only miracle. Is it possible that the Qur'an is a miracle because of its eloquence when it really *lacks* that eloquence in many verses and paragraphs?

On the other hand, if we compare the Qur'an to the seven famous Arabic poems called the "Hanging Poems," the Qur'an's position would have to be #8 in rhetoric and eloquence — after we forget about its huge grammatical and historical mistakes! These were the poems etched on the Ka'aba unto this day, which were presented to Muhammad by the people of Mecca as the works that he could not even come *close* to matching.

Inspiration of Muhammad's Companions?

More evidence that proves that the Qur'an is man-made and not heavenly is this fact: ***many of its verses did not come down from heaven***, but rather ***came up*** from Muhammad's companions and his wives. Were, therefore, Abu Bakr and Umar Al-Khattab also prophets for their active participation in the writing of the Qur'an? Who knows? Let us see…

Abu Bakr

One Sura says:

> "Muhammad is no more than a Messenger; many were the Messengers that passed away before him. If he died or was slain, will ye then turn back on your heels? If any did turn back on his heels, not the least harm will he do to Allah, but Allah will reward the grateful."[200]

---

200) Sura *Al-Imran* (the Family of Imran) 3:144, author's translation.

In speaking about that verse, the famous Muslim Imam, Muhammad bin Abd Al-Wahab wrote:

> "Abu Bakr came and entered the mosque; that was when he heard the news (the death of Muhammad), as Umar was preoccupied in his grief addressing the people from the pulpit, and he did not realize who was coming in. In the meantime, Ali entered the house of Aisha where Muhammad was lying dead. He approached him, uncovered his face, and he kissed him. Then Ali said: 'By my father and my mother, you have tasted the death that Allah has predestined for you, and you will suffer no other death.' Then Ali covered back his face, and went out to the Mosque. He tried to address the people, but Umar insisted on continuing his speech. But when Abu Bakr saw that Umar was not about to stop speaking, he, himself, began to speak, interrupting Umar, and the people turn towards him and left Umar. There, Abu Bakr thanked Allah the all-mighty and praised him, and said to the people, 'To those who worshipped Muhammad, now, Muhammad died. But to those who worship Allah, Allah is alive and will never die.'"[201]

Then he included the above quoted verse (Sura 3:144) as a part of his speech. Ibn Ishaq quoted Ibn Al-Zuhairi:

> "Sa'id Ibn Al-Musayyeb told me quoting Abi Hurayra who said: 'By Allah, the people never knew that that verse came down until Abu Bakr recited it on that day.' Then the people took it from Abu Bakr. Abu Kurayra said that Umar confirmed: "By Allah, I have never heard it until Abu Bakr recited it."

Where did Abu Bakr come up with that verse, when it

---

201) *The Life of the Prophet* by Muhammad bin Abd Al-Wahab, p. 145.

did not originally come down to Muhammad? Nobody ever hear Muhammad recite that verse. Did he recite it secretly to Abu Bakr only? If he did, why? Was Abu Bakr suddenly a prophet, with verses coming down upon him, after the death of Muhammad? Nobody knows.

Umar Ibn Al-Khattab

Abu Bakr was not alone in receiving verses that came down upon him. Umar Ibn Al-Khattab said a statement that "Gabriel" immediately adopted and brought down to Muhammad. Al-Bukhari, in his **Sahih**,[202] quoted in **Al-Ittiqan**:

> "Umar said: My Lord has agreed with me on three. I said: Messenger of Allah, O that we take of Abraham's shrine as a place for prayer. And the verse came down: 'Take unto yourselves of Abraham's shrine a place of prayer.' Then, I said: O Messenger of Allah, the righteous and the wicked enter the houses of your wives. O that you command them to cover. The verse of the Hijab (the cover) came down. And one time, the wives of Allah's Messenger rose up against him, and I said to them, his god may order you divorced from him and he may give him instead wives that are better than you. These very words came down in the Sura of Al-Tahrim 66:5."[203]

To be specific about the verses that were inspired by Umar, most Muslim scholars, not just Al-Suyuti, have acknowledged them.[204] However, Al-Baydawi made things much clearer when he wrote:

---

202) See the *Hadith* of Sahih Bukhari, Vol. 1, Book 8, #395 and Vol. 6, Book 60, #10.
203) *Al-Ittiqan* by Al-Suyuti, Vol. I, p. 99.
204) See *Al-Baydawi*, p. 26, *1l*, p. 18, *Al-Kashaf* by Al-Zamkhashri, Vol. I, p. 31; and *Sahih Al-Mustanad*.

"Muhammad took the hand of Umar and said to him, 'This is the shrine of Abraham.' Umar said to him, 'Shouldn't you take it as a place of prayer (a mosque)?' Muhammad said to him, 'I was not commanded from Allah to do so.' But Allah commanded him to do so, that very same day."

Another incident mentioned by Al-Suyuti shows how the revelation of Muhammad was caused:

"A Jew met Umar Ibn Al-Khattab. The Jew argued with him and attempted to convince him that Muhammad was not a prophet and that "Gabriel" who spoke to him was only an enemy of the Jews. Umar answered him, 'Whoever was the enemy of Allah, of the angels, of his messengers, of "Gabriel" and of Michael, for Allah is the enemy of the unbelievers.' Just two days later, that saying came down as a verse that is now found in the Qur'an, Sura of the Cow 2:98."[205]

Did Allah send down the revelation to Umar then, instead of Muhammad? Or did it come down upon Muhammad?

Zayd bin Thabit

Another story was told by Zayd, one of the writers of the revelation of Muhammad (the Qur'an). He said:

"Muhammad sent for me and said to me, write down what my Lord has sent down upon me, 'Those who are seated down in the faith cannot be equal to those who are struggling in the cause of Allah.' Among those who were present at the time he was dictating that to me, was Ibn Umm Kulthum, who was a blind man. He said to the Messenger of Allah, 'But I am

---

205) *Al-Ittiqan* by Al-Suyuti, Vol. I, p. 100.

blind.' Then Muhammad said to Zayd, 'Add to that verse, 'except those who have a disability.'"[206]

Was that a heavenly revelation or spontaneous advice? I leave it to you to decide.

Abd Allah bin Sa'd

Abd Allah bin Sa'd, another writer used by Muhammad, left Muhammad because he discovered there was no revelation and no "Gabriel." He said:

> "Muhammad used to say to me to write at the end of every section: 'Allah is dear and wise.' But I wrote: 'forgiving, merciful.' Muhammad would respond: 'It is the same, anyway.'"[207]

Consequently, bin Sa'd left Islam. He ran away because Muhammad threatened to kill him after he was told what bin Sa'd said:

> "If Allah sent down the revelation upon Muhammad, He must have then sent it down upon me, also. Whenever Muhammad said, 'Allah heareth and knoweth all,' I wrote, 'Allah is all knowing and wise.' His usual response was: 'bin Sa'd, write whatever you want.'"

In response to the charges of bin Sa'd, the following verse came down upon Muhammad, *Al-An'am* (the Cattle) 6:93:

> "Who can be more wicked than one who inventeth a lie against Allah or saith: 'I have received inspiration,' when he hath received none, or who saith: I can reveal the like of what Allah hath revealed"?[208]

---

206) See *Al-Baydawi*, p. 123; *Al-Kashaf* by Al-Zamkhashri, Vol. I, p. 53; *Al-Ittiqan* by Al-Suyuti, p. 98; *Sahih Al-Mustanad*, p. 53; and *The Causes of the Revelation* by Al-Wahidi, p. 98.
207) See *The Causes of Descendancy* by Al-Suyuti, pp. 12 & 121.
208) Sura *Al-An'am* (the Cattle) 6:93.

As usual, "Gabriel" was ready with a verse to justify the actions of Muhammad as he spilled the blood of bin Sa'd.

Umm Salma

Umm Salma, one of Muhammad's wives, once asked:

> "O Messenger of Allah, I have never heard the mention of women during the Hijra (the flight to and the stay in Medina)."

Immediately, this verse conveniently came down:

> "And their Lord hath accepted of them, and answered them: Never will I suffer to be lost the work of any of you, be he male or a female; ye are members, one of another."[209]

Then Umm Salma added:

> "O Messenger of Allah, you mention only the men, but not the women."

As always, "Gabriel" was ready. This verse came down:

> "For Muslim men and women, for believing men and women, for devout men and women, for true men and women, for men and women who are patient and constant ..." etc.[210]

Many more Suras came down from "Gabriel" to satisfy Muhammad's wives and companions.[211]

Aisha

In another situation, Aisha, the spoiled wife of Muhammad, said:

---

209) Sura *Al-Imran* (the Family of Imran) 3:195.

210) Sura *Al-Ahzab* (the Allies) 33:35.

211) For instance, see *Al-Baydawi*, pp. 100 & 558; *Al-Kashaf* by Al-Zamkhashri, Vol. I, p. 490; *Al-Jalalayn*, p. 353; *Sahih Al-Sanad*, p. 120; *Al-Ittiqan* by Al-Suyuti, pp. 69 & 219; and *The Causes of Descendancy* by Al-Wahidi, p. 268.

"I was with Allah's Messenger during one of his raids. He as usual had sex with me, every night. But when the morning came, he did not find water to wash in order to pray. I said to him: 'Muhammad, aren't we created out of sand?' And he said, 'Yes.' I said, 'Then, why then is this confusion, you and the men need the water and cannot find it, the sand is always there. Use it.'"

As usual, "Gabriel" came down immediately with a verse[212] that permitted the use of sand (called in Arabic, *Al-Tayammum*) to prepare for praying, instead of water.[213]

How can sand clean men enough to pray, when sand adds to dirtiness, and never helps clean? Yet those were the wishes of Muhammad and his lord. (In fact, those were the wishes of Aisha.) But it does not matter whose wishes they were, as long as there are men who are ready to agree to anything Muhammad said, with no questions asked.

Muhammad's Maid?

Muhammad's manipulation of his lord and of "Gabriel" was not limited to important affairs, but extended to trivial matters. For example, because a small puppy dog died under Muhammad's bed, "Gabriel" stopped coming down with verses upon Muhammad. Muhammad sought the help of his maid, asking her: "What happened, Khawla, that "Gabriel" stopped coming down upon me?' (First, this indicates that a few days had passed since the death of the dog. By

212) See *An-Nisa'* (the Women) 4:43.
213) See *Al-Ittiqan* by Al-Suyuti, p. 101; and *Al-Jalalayn*, p. 89. A different version is found in the *Hadith* of Sahih Bukhari, Vol. 1, Book 7, #330 & 332; Vol. 5, Book 57, #21; Vol. 6, Book 60, #101 & 131; Vol. 7, Book 62, #93 & Book 72, #770; Vol. 8, Book 82, #827; the *Hadith* of Sahih Muslim, Book 3, Chapter 27, "Tayammum," #714-715; the *Sunan Abu-Dawud* Book 1, # 317; and *Malik's Muwatta*, Book 2, #2.24.91.

then the dead dog should have stunk.) Also, was it logical for a prophet to ask a maid why an angel stopped delivering his message? Come on!

Khawla decided to clean the room, and when she cleaned under the bed, she found the dead dog. (How could Muhammad not smell a dog that had been dead under his bed for several days? Who can believe a story like this? Hundreds of millions!)

Right after his room was cleaned, Muhammad's god sent down Sura *Ad-Duha* (the Early Hours) 93:5.[214] Was Allah incapable of keeping the dog alive while it was in Muhammad's house, so "Gabriel" could enter to deliver his messages? Couldn't Muhammad's god send him the verses while he was outside his room, or at another of his many houses? One cannot make logical sense out of that story.

Another Source for Inspiration

Al-Suyuti wrote:

> "Ibn Abbas said that there was a woman who prayed behind the Prophet, and she was beautiful. Some people came to the front lines of prayer and others stood in the back rows. However, when Muhammad knelt, he peeked at the beautiful woman from under his armpit."[215]

For this, a verse came down: [216]

> "To Us are known those of you who hastened forward, and those who lag behind."[217]

---

214) This was also recorded in *Al-Ittiqan* by Al-Baydawi, p. 802; and *The Causes of Descendancy* by Al-Wahidi, p. 338.

215) See *Al-Ittiqan* by Al-Suyuti, p. 159.

216) Sura *Al-Hijr* (the Rock) 15:24.

217) This story was confirmed by *Al-Baydawi*, p. 346; *Al-Kashaf* by Al-Zamkhashri, Vol. II, p. 576; and mentioned by Ibn Majeh and Al-Tabari.

Later, Muslim scholars claimed that by this verse the Qur'an was laying the foundation for the future criterion as to how Muslim men and women should pray separated. What foundation could be laid by that verse when we see Muslim pilgrims, men and women, go around half naked during the hajj season, roaming in a place they believe to be most holy? They are *still* praying side by side, in front of each other and behind each other! Look at this verse:

"No prophet could (ever) be false to his trust."[218]

Al-Baydawi explained why that verse came down. He said that a piece of red velvet, which was looted by Muslims in one of the raids, was lost. The Muslims accused the prophet of taking it. Consequently, Muhammad's god came to his aid, and he sent down that verse to justify him, as usual.[219]

Could that verse be applicable to all ages and all places? Their interpretation, that the Qur'an is applicable to all generations, is full of holes. I hope that Muslims will weigh those verses with a sound mind, not "weighing them in the balances" of unreasonable and gullible logic.

In conclusion, the Qur'an reads:

"O ye who believe! When ye are told to make room in the assemblies, (spread out and) make room: ample room will Allah provide for you."[220]

Al-Suyuti said that verse came down because...

"The words of the kings cannot be unheeded or ignored."[221]

That means the words of the king could not be canceled,

---

218) Sura *Al-Imran* (the Family of Imran) 3:161

219) This is also found in the *Sunan Abu-Dawud*, Book 30, #3960.

220) Sura *Al-Mujadilah* (She Who Pleaded) 58:11, Yusuf Ali.

221) *The Causes of Descendancy* by Al-Suyuti, p. 265.

even though the king was a human, a servant of God. However, Muhammad and his Qur'an say that it is possible for the God who created man to give a command or send down a verse and then cancel it. It was as if Muhammad's god had been hasty in sending it down, or was too busy with other things to realize he had made a mistake. So he sent down "Gabriel" with a *new* command or a *new* verse to cancel his mistake! (Oops!) Could this be the act of the Holy God?

"The Annulling and the Annulled" and Contradictions in the Qur'an:

In this section, we will discuss both contradictions in the Qur'an, and the dangerous practice of one verse replacing another verse, as though Allah said, "Oops, I made a mistake and I need to correct it." This practice in the Qur'an is known as "The Annulling and the Annulled" (الناسخ والمنسوخ).

Contradictions in the Qur'an

More than 25% of the Qur'an verses contradict each other. A few examples will be discussed here.

No Compulsion in Religion?

"Let there be no compulsion in religion. Truth stands out clear from error: whoever rejects evil and believes in Allah hath grasped the most trustworthy hand-hold, that never breaks. And Allah heareth and knoweth all things."[222]

The Qur'an reveals through that verse that there is liberty for men to choose their faith. Another verse confirms this:

"Say unto those who received the Book, and unto the gentiles, have you accepted Islam? If they have accepted Islam, then they have been guided (to the truth); but if they rejected, then all that was required

222) Sura *Al-Baqara* (the Cow) 2:256.

of you is to let them know. And Allah is all-seeing
all of his creatures."[223]

A third verse that proves there should be liberty in choosing one's faith says:

"Thy duty is to make (the message) reach them. It is
our part to call them to account."[224]

A fourth verse teaches liberty in choosing one's faith:

"And those who take as protectors others beside him
—Allah doth watch over them, and thou art not the
disposer of their affairs."[225]

However, the Qur'an could not keep tolerating the freedom to choose one's faith. When Muhammad grabbed the
authority and possessed much power, he suddenly changed
his attitude on liberty, as revealed in the Sura of the Cow:

"And fight them on until there is no more resistance,
and religion will be Allah's. But if they desisted, there
will be no aggression except against the oppressors."[226]

Allah commands fighting against those who do not accept Muhammad's religion:

"Fight those who believe not in Allah nor the last
day, nor hold that forbidden which hath been forbidden by Allah and his Messenger, nor acknowledge the religion of truth, (even if they are) of the
people of the Book, until they pay the Jizya (taxes),[227]
with willing submission, and feel themselves subdued."[228]

---

223) Sura *Al-Imran* (the Family of Imran) 3:20, author's translation.

224) Sura *Ar-Ra'd* (the Thunder) 13:40.

225) Sura *Ash-Shura* (the Counsel) 42:6.

226) Sura *Al-Baqara* (the Cow) 2:193, author's translation.

227) *Jizya* – taxes/tribute paid in return for not being slain by Muslims.

228) Sura *At-Tauba* (Repentance) 9:29.

A third confirmation from Muhammad's god to fight the unbelievers, came in the same Sura:

> "O Prophet! Strive hard against the unbelievers and the hypocrites, and be firm against them. Their abode is hell — an evil refuge indeed."[229]

The Qur'an commands:

> "They but wish that ye should reject Faith, as they do, and thus be on the same footing (as they); but take not friends from their ranks until they flee in the way of Allah. But if they turn renegades, seize them and slay them wherever ye find them; and take no friends or helpers from their ranks."[230]

Any reader can easily see the clear contradictions in those verses. Who can comprehend why Muhammad's god changed his mind so easily and so drastically? Even Muhammad contradicted the Qur'anic verses concerning the freedom of choice, in the *Hadith*, when he said:

> "I was commanded to fight the people until they say, No god but Allah and Muhammad is the Messenger of Allah."[231]

In all, the Qur'an contains more than 220 contradictions.

Contradictions: The Qur'an Came Down in Arabic

The following Qur'anic verses emphasize that the text of the Qur'an came down upon Muhammad in the Arabic language: Suras *Ibrahim* 14:4; *Ash-Shu'ara* 26:195; *Ar-Ra'd* 13:37; *An-Nahl* 16:103; and *Ha Mim Sajda* 41:44.[232] All those verses came down to make sure that Arabic is the lan-

---

229) Sura *At-Tauba* (Repentance) 9:73.
230) Sura *An-Nisa'* (the Women) 4:89.
231) The *Hadith* of Sahih Bukhari, Vol. 1, Book 2, #24. See Chapter 4, Footnote #66 for more references.
232) See Chapter 5, Footnote #13 for more references.

guage of the Qur'an, and that it has no letter in it that came
in other than the Arabic language. However, Al-Suyuti confirmed that there are 118 words in the Qur'an that are *not*
Arabic.[233] Ibn Abbas also confirmed that there are Persian,
Ethiopian, Nubian and Turkish words in the Qur'an. Even
the word, *Issa* (Jesus), is not an Arabic word!

Contradictions: The Day of the Resurrection

Here are some contradictions in the Qur'an concerning
the resurrection day. Ibn Abbas said that one day an Arabian
mentioned to him that the Qur'an writes that the length
of the Day of the Resurrection is a period of one thousand
years, as recorded in Sura *As-Sajdah* 32:5. On the other hand,
in Sura *Al-Ma'arij* 70:4, and another place, it gives its length
as 50,000 years. Abu Abbas answered that those two days
and the periods they represent are mentioned in the Qur'an,
but Allah is the one who knows the real answer about them
(a defeatist's way to dodge an embarrassment).

Other contradictions

Here I will simply display the verse, followed by another
that contradicts and annuls it:

1. Sura *Al-Mu'minun* 23:101:

   "There will be no more relationships between them
   that day, nor will one ask after another."

In direct contradiction, *As-Saffat* 37:27 says:

   "And they will turn to one another, and question one
   another."

2. Sura *As-Sajdah* 32:4:

   "It is Allah who has created the heavens and the
   earth, and all between them, in six days."

---

233) See *Al-Ittiqan* by Al-Suyuti, Vol. II, pp. 108-109.

In direct contradiction, *Ha Mim Sajdah* 41:9 reads:

"Say, Is it that ye deny him who created the earth <u>in two days</u>? And do ye join equals with him? He is the lord of the worlds."

3. Sura *An-Nisa'* 4:3:

"... Marry women of your choice, two, three, or four; but if ye fear that ye shall not be able to deal justly (with them), then only one...."

In the above verse, the Qur'an is teaching that there is a possibility of dealing justly with women, but it contradicts itself *in the same Sura*:

"Ye are never able to be fair and just as among women, even if it is your ardent desire...." (4:129)

4. Sura *Al-A'raf* 7:28 says:

"...Nay, Allah never commands what is shameful..."

But in *Bani Isra'il* 17:16 the Qur'an clearly contradicts itself, quoting Allah:

"When We decide to destroy a population, We (first) send a definite order to those among them who are given the good things of life and yet transgress, so that they commit shameful abominations in it, so that the word is proved true against them, then We destroy them utterly."[234]

Did not the god of Muhammad, in this verse, command the rich people of that city to commit the shameful acts so that he can destroy them? Did the Qur'an contradict itself?

6. Sura *Ar-Ra'd* 13:28 describes the believers:

"Those who believe, and whose hearts find satisfaction in the remembrance of Allah...."

---

234) This verse is partly the author's own translation.

But Sura *Al-Anfal* 8:2 contradicts the above verse:

"For believers are those who, when Allah is mentioned, feel a tremor in their hearts...."

7. In Sura *Al-Balad* 90:1, Muhammad says he did not swear by "this city" (Mecca):

"I do not swear by this city."[235]

Then he contradicts that verse in *At-Tin* 95:1-3:

"(I swear) by the fig, and by the olive, and by the Mount of Sinai, and by this city of security."[236]

By the way, how could a prophet of God swear by figs and olives? That is funny for anyone to do, let alone someone who calls himself a prophet!

8. However, the contradiction of the highest significance regards the crucifixion of Christ. Was He killed or not?

Sura *An-Nisa'* 4:157 says:

"That they (the Jews) said (in boast), 'We killed Christ Jesus, the son of Mary, the Apostle of God,' but they killed Him not, nor crucified Him, but so it was made to appear to them, and those who differ therein are full of doubts, with no (certain) knowledge, but only conjecture to follow, for of a surety, they killed him not."

Muslims always quote this verse in reply to Christians' claim of the crucifixion of Christ. In such response, Muslims forget Sura *Al-Imran* 3:55:

"Behold! Allah said, O Jesus, I will cause thee to die[237]

---

235) Author's own translation, agreeing with Rodwell (1876) and Palmer (1880).

236) Author's own translation, agreeing with Rodwell.

237) Author's own translation, agreeing with Rodwell. Rodwell explains why this translation is correct in his footnote.

and raise thee to myself, and clear thee (of the false-hoods) of those who blaspheme; I will make those who follow thee superior to those who disbelieve (in you), even to the day of the Resurrection. Then shall ye all return unto me, and I will judge between you of the matters wherein ye dispute."

Here, the Qur'an not only mentions the death of Christ, contradicting the previous verse, but also declares that who-ever follows Christ is superior to any other person on the Judgment Day! The Qur'an also mentions the death of Christ in Sura *Maryam* 19:33:

"So peace is on me, the day I was born, the day I die, and the day that I shall be raised up to life (again)."

Here are *two* verses in the Qur'an speaking of the death of Christ, and *one* verse that said that He did not die!

Did Muhammad have two gods: one who told him Christ would die; and the other god who told him Christ would *not* die? How could that be, when Muhammad said: "There is no god but Allah"? He insists that God is absolutely one, not two. Then why are there all those contradictions?

Historical Mistakes

There are too many contradictions in the Qur'an! How could Muhammad's god contradict himself so frequently? We can add to that the linguistic mistakes, and the many *historical* mistakes when Muhammad tried to refer to Bible history. Historical events Muhammad mentions in his Qur'an are a total fabrication, not mentioned in the Bible or anywhere else. It should be noted that when Muhammad referred to a Bible story, he never quoted from the Bible. He simply made up events as he went along.

1. The Gospels do not mention that the Virgin Mary had

a brother. But the god of Muhammad said in the Qur'an, addressing the Virgin Mary: "O sister of Aaron..." (*Maryam* 19:28). In other words, Muhammad gave Mary a brother the Bible never says she had.

2. While on that subject, the Qur'an says Mary was the sister of Aaron, and that her father was Imran. But wait a minute. Aaron and Imran (Amram) were of the tribe of Levi. Mary was of the tribe of *Judah*. What's more, Aaron and Imran lived 1,500 years before Christ! It would be a *little* difficult for those two men to be Mary's father and her brother! Besides, the Bible says the father of Mary was Heli[238] and definitely not Imran.

3. Another historical mistake in the Qur'an is the story of Abraham. It says that Abraham came out of Hebron, accompanied by Hagar and Ishmael, to go to Mecca, where he left them, and returned to Hebron where his wife Sarah was waiting for him. The Bible says that Hagar and her son left Hebron alone and went south to Beersheba, where she was lost and the angel of God saved them. A few years later, Hagar arranged for her son to marry an Egyptian.[239] This could not have happened if Ishmael was in Mecca. If the Qur'an is true, how did Abraham travel about 1000 miles on foot through the burning sand of the barren desert?

4. A third mistake: the Qur'an says the well of Zamzam, in Mecca, sprang under the feet of Ishmael. But the truth is: the well of Beersheba that sprang was a bowshot from Ishmael[240], not the well of Zamzam, and not "under his feet."

5. The Qur'an makes other huge historical mistakes. It says that Haman was the Egyptian Pharaoh's minister. But

---

238) See Luke 4:23.
239) See Genesis 21:14-21.
240) See Genesis 21:16 & 19.

Haman was the minister of Ahasuerus in Shushan which was in Persia;[241] i.e., 400s BC Iran, not 1400s BC Egypt.

6. The Qur'an mentions that it was the *wife* of Pharaoh who found Moses in the Nile River, when the Bible tells us that it was Pharaoh's *daughter* who found Moses.[242]

7. The Qur'an teaches that it was a man called "The Samaritan" who molded the cow to be the idol of Israel in the wilderness. But it is well-known that the Samaritans came to Israel after the Babylonian Captivity in the sixth century BC.[243] Further, the Bible tells us that the person who carved the idol for Israel was Aaron, the brother of Moses.[244]

8. Another big mistake in the Qur'an is where it says that Jesus was born under a palm tree,[245] where he spoke a few minutes after His birth, saying:

"And shake towards thyself the trunk of the palm tree: it will be fall fresh ripe (date fruits) upon thee."[246]

First, Jesus was born in a stable, not under the palm tree. Second, the dates could not be ripe and ready at the season of Christ's birth. Besides, the mountainous area of Bethlehem does not allow the growth of palm tees. Palm trees need areas where the weather is hot, such as semi-desert areas.

9. In his explanation of lightning and thunder, Muhammad stated:

"The thunder and lightning are two of Allah's angels." The Qur'an says thunder is a praise of Allah.[247]

241) See the Book of Esther.
242) See Exodus 2:5-10.
243) See 2 Kings 17:24.
244) See Exodus 32:2-4.
245) See Sura *Maryam* (Mary) 19:23.
246) Sura *Maryam* (Mary) 19:25.
247) See Sura *Ar-Ra'd* (the Thunder) 13:13.

Al-Baydawi wrote in his interpretation of the Sura of The Thunder:

> "Ibn Abbas asked the Messenger of Allah about the thunder, and he (Muhammad) answered him: 'It is the angel of Allah who is responsible for the clouds, and he has torches of fire that he uses to drive the clouds.'"[248]

However, Al-Suyuti wrote that Ibn Abbas said:

> "Some Jews came to Muhammad and asked him: 'Tell us about the thunder.' And he answered them, 'He is one of the angels of Allah who chases away the clouds with a torch of fire, and drives them to wherever Allah commands.' They asked him, 'And what is this noise that we hear?' He answered them, 'That noise is his (that angel's) noise.'"[249]

Muhammad gave names to some of the important angels, like "Gabriel," Michael, Harut, Marut,[250] Azrael (the angel of death), the Thunder, and the Lightning. Muhammad also taught that Lightning is an angel with four faces.

10. The Qur'an claims Alexander the Great was a pious man, and Muhammad almost made him a prophet, when it was well known historically that Alexander was a heathen who worshipped idols. He even let himself be called Amon, after an Egyptian god.

11. Here, we put before Muslim scholars what Muhammad said concerning the sun at sunset. The Qur'an states:

> "They ask thee concerning Zul-qarnain[251] (Alexan-

---

248) This was confirmed in *Al-Jalalayn* by Jalal & Jalal, p. 602.

249) *Al-Ittiqan* by Al-Suyuti, Vol. IV, p. 230.

250) *Harut* and *Marut* are 2 legendary angels that deceived the people of Babel, according to Sura *Al-Baqara* (the Cow) 2:102.

251) The term means, "The Two-Horned One."

der as known in Arabic history), Say, I will rehearse to you something of his story. Verily, We established his power on earth, and We gave him the ways and the means to all ends. ... Until when he reached the setting of the sun, he found it set in a spring of murky water; near it he found a people."[252]

Excuse me!?! Jalal & Jalal said in their interpretation of this verse that the setting of the sun was in a spring that has black clay in it.[253] But Al-Baydawi's interpretation of Sura *Ya Sin* 36:38 was in this manner:

"The sun runs to settle down in a place that is hers, and that is the decision of the dear, wise Allah."

He continued on to say that the sun runs for a certain distance before it settles down, and it becomes like a traveler who walks a certain distance.[254] Al-Zamkhashri said:

"Aba Zurr was with Muhammad when the sun was going down, he ask him, 'Where does this go down to (pointing at the sun)?' Then, he continued, 'Allah and His Messenger know well.' Muhammad answered, 'It sets down in a hot (حامية) spring.'"[255]

Ibn Abbas said not hot but (حمئة) black clay (meaning volcanic).

Many questions are raised here. Does the sun take a nap, as travelers do, so that it can get the rest it needs before it comes back to the skies again? Or what happens when the sun sets? How could the sun plunge into a pond of black mud? Was Muhammad's god so incapable of telling him the

---

252) Sura *Al-Kahf* (the Cave) 18:83-84, 86.
253) See *Al-Jalalayn* by Jalal & Jalal, p. 251 and *Al-Tabari*, p. 339.
254) See *Al-Baydawi*, pp. 584-585; and *Al-Ittiqan* by Al-Suyuti, Vol. IV, p. 242.
255) *Al-Kashaf* by Al-Zamkhashri, Vol. II, p. 742.

truth about the sun and the sunset? It is now clear that the interpretations of Muslim scholars do not need any comment. Moreover, the words of Muhammad would not be acceptable to modern scientists because they are totally void of sound logic.

12. The earth, as far as the Qur'an is concerned, is flat and stands on some columns. Moreover, the Qur'an claims that the earth is stretched:

> "And at the earth, how it is spread out (how it was made flat)."[256]

The Qur'an also says:

> "And we have set on the earth mountains standing firm (real translation: We have set in the earth anchors), lest it should shake with them. And we have made therein broad highways (canyons) for them to pass through, that they may receive guidance."[257]

In another Sura, it says:

> "And the mountains hath he firmly fixed (hath he anchored)."[258]

This story is repeated:

> "And the earth, We have spread it out, and set thereon mountains standing firm (and thrown in it anchors)...."[259]

In Muhammad's mind, the anchors were needed so the earth would not wave and shake. Before taking a scientific look at those verses, let us look at the interpretation of these learned Muslim scholars. Jalal & Jalal wrote:

---

256) Sura *Al-Ghashiya* (the Overwhelming Calamity) 88:20.
257) Sura *Al-Anbiya'* (the Prophets) 21:31
258) Sura *An-Nazi'at* (Those Who Pull Out) 79:32
259) Sura *Qaf* 50:7

"Allah put in the earth firm anchors, of the fear that it would lean with all the people on it."[260]

Was that a joke? Later they wrote that his saying, "it was made flat" indicates that the earth is flat."[261] Many Muslim scholars have agreed with that comment.

13. Moreover, the Qur'an ascertains that the earth is set over some pillars so it will not lose its stability with all the people on it. I remember as a child, that many Muslim scholars and their Imams said the earth is flat; and anyone who believed otherwise was a blasphemer. I am talking about Muslims who taught this less than forty years ago!

After we entered the space age, astronauts and cosmonauts went to the moon. They took pictures of the earth from outer space and we discovered, without any doubt, that the earth is a globe and not flat. Could it be that in Muhammad's day the earth had columns to support it and was flat; but now, God gave us a new heaven and a new earth that are totally different from the earth described in the Qur'an? I would like those who are educated Muslims to give us an answer.

These are some of the scientific mistakes the Qur'an recorded, listed only to prove that it could not be a book from God. Had it been from God, the "facts of nature" mentioned in it would have been true. Furthermore, even though the Qur'an quoted the Bible, it did it inaccurately. It could not refer to facts as they were recorded in the Bible. For example, the Bible stated clearly that the earth was round, a globe, in the eighth century BC – about a thousand years before Muhammad. Isaiah wrote about the globe of the earth:

"It is He who sitteth upon the circle of the earth…"[262]

---

260) *Al-Jalalayn* by Jalal & Jalal, p. 271
261) *Al-Jalalayn*, p. 509.
262) Isaiah 40:22.

The Bible came hundreds of years before the Qur'an, yet the differences are many and major. But Muslims are excused, for the God of the Bible is *not* the god of the Qur'an! When will my people wake up?

"The Annulling and the Annulled"

Next we will concentrate on the "The Annulling and the Annulled" in the Qur'an. This means that Muhammad had the right to delete and cancel verses of the Qur'an at will.

Some critics have claimed that the god of Muhammad would often recite verses, then, after a short period of time, he would cancel or delete them. Some verses of the Qur'an were canceled or changed only a few hours after coming down upon Muhammad. How did Muhammad treat this problem, and how did he justify his actions in this regard?

Allah Will Substitute Something Better?

At one point the whole calling and mission of Muhammad was almost a total failure. The Jews of Arabia doubled their efforts in attacking Muhammad and his teachings, claiming that after Muhammad issued a command to his followers, he would withdraw it a little later. However Muhammad found, as usual, a god who was ever ready to send "Gabriel" with a verse to help him out of his dilemma, and assure people that it was Allah, not Muhammad who ordered the deleting. The verse came down, as though Allah was saying:

> "If any of our revelation (verses) do we abrogate, or cause to be forgotten; We (Allah) will substitute (it with) something better or similar (to it). Knowest thou not that Allah hath power over all things?"[263]

According to Al-Suyuti, "Abrogation means deleting or

---

263) See Sura *Baqara* (the Cow) 2:106.

canceling."[264] Abrogation means changing, as it is used in Sura *Al-Hajj* 22:52. Dr. Ahmed Shalabi wrote that abrogation means blotting out something and replacing it with something else.[265]

We were told that the Qur'an is good and applicable to all ages and all places. We were told that it is "the Word of God." **But why was Muhammad's god so *incompetent* that he felt obligated to change his own words?** He is supposed to be God – a god who was supposed to know what he was doing, my dear Muslim friends. How could God change His words, for better or worse? How?

"Lightening" Allah's Commands?

Muhammad's god sent down verses to "lighten" some obligations that he earlier commanded to be performed. For example, the god that commanded and urged people to pray four times during the night, between sunset and sunrise (something confirmed by several Qur'anic verses and many of the sayings of Muhammad in the *Hadith*), changed his mind shortly thereafter. He also changed his mind concerning praying at night, as it was recorded in *Al-Muzammil*:

"O thou folded in garments! Stand (to prayer) by night, but not all night …"[266]

Then he showed that Allah retracted His words:

"… Read ye, therefore, of the Qur'an as much as may be easy (for you) …."[267]

Why was the load of praying at night lessened? It was the wives of Muhammad! Whenever he entered their homes at night, he found them praying, according to the Qur'an. So

264) *Al-Ittiqan* by Al-Suyuti, Vol. II, p. 9.
265) *The History of Islamic Legislation* by Ahmed Shalabi, page 115
266) Sura *Al-Muzammil* (the Mantled One) 73:1-2.
267) Sura *Al-Muzammil*, 73:20.

he received a new revelation amending the earlier revelation, as though to accommodate his lusts. And Muslims audaciously accuse Christians of altering the Bible? By the way, there has never been one case of "Annulling-and-Annulled" in the Bible. But the Qur'an was openly and often changed. What do Muslim scholars say about changing revelation within the Qur'an?

What Is the "Whole Qur'an"?

Umar Ibn Al-Khattab, the second successor after Muhammad, said:

> "Let no one of you say that I have received the whole Qur'an, for who knows what is the whole Qur'an? For much of it has ceased to exist; but let him say that I have received (of the Qur'an) what has been revealed."[268]

Aisha, known as the Mother of the Believers and the wife of Muhammad, said that Sura *Al-Ahzab*[269] used to be...

> "in the days of the Prophet, two hundred verses; but when 'Uthman, the third successor, collected the Qur'an, only 73 verses were found in it."

Ibn Banu Ka'b, one of Muhammad's companions, asked one Muslim, "How many verses are in Sura *Al-Ahzab*?" He answered, "73." Ibn Ka'b said there were 286, the same as the Sura of the Cow.[270] "Do you include the verse [on stoning adulterers] in Sura *Al-Ahzab*?" He said, "No." Then, Umar confirmed the validity of that verse, and said he was planning to add it to the Qur'an after he became a Caliph.[271]

---

268) *Al-Ittiqan* by Al-Suyuti, Vol. III, p. 72.

269) Sura 33, *Al-Ahzab* (the Allies).

270) Sura 2, *Al-Baqara* (the Cow).

271) Stated by Al-Suyuti. This fact was further confirmed in *The Causes of the Revelation* by Al-Wahidi, p. 13.

Nullified by Chickens?

Many verses were added to the Qur'an immediately after Muhammad's death. And many other verses were deleted by 'Uthman ibn 'Affan, who ordered it refined and had the accents put on its letters. But where did all those deleted Suras and verses go? We can even ask: Where did the Qur'an of Muhammad go? According to Ibn Hazm, Aisha said some of the verses, such as those of the stoning and the suckling,[272] which were in some of the pages she had, were eaten by chickens as she was preoccupied by the death of Muhammad.[273] 'Abdullah bin Abu Bakr seconded Aisha's story.

Some Muslim scholars may claim that the verses which were eaten by chickens had been nullified. But of course, they really do not know for sure because they were not with the chickens when they ate the verses. But how could those verses be nullified after Muhammad had already died? And how could chickens nullify those verses, when some of those verses that were eaten are still in the Qur'an?

Moreover, Umar insisted on adding to the Qur'an the verse of the suckling after he heard Aisha reciting it. He almost added the verse on stoning too, after he heard it recited by Ka'b. But worse yet, where did the *two hundred verses* of the Sura *Al-Ahzab* go? Were they *also* eaten by chickens? Didn't Muhammad's god say:

> "We have sent down the Message, and we will surely guard it from corruption"?[274]

How then did Muhammad's lord not guard his words and

---

272) *Stoning and Suckling* – verses not in the present Qur'an. However, many verses on both subjects are in the *Ahadith*.
273) This was confirmed by *Ibn Hazm*, Vol. III, part 11, pp. 235-236; *Al-Kashaf* by Al-Zamkhashri, p. 518 and other Muslim scholars.
274) See Sura *Al-Hijr* (the Rock) 15:9.

his Qur'an from those chickens? Couldn't that god prohibit chickens from devouring his Qur'anic verses? Or couldn't he prohibit 'Uthman from deleting *hundreds* of verses from the Qur'an? Dr. Mousa Al-Mousawi, a contemporary Iranian scholar, stated:

> "Those who say that there is alteration in the Qur'an, form a part of all the Islamic groups, However, the Shiite scholars form the greatest percentage of them."[275]

That is a blatant confession of trusted Muslim scholars, confirmed by Al-Mousawi, admitting that the Qur'an has been tampered with and changed.

Missing Verses – and Missing Suras?

So many verses were deleted from the Sura 33 (*Al-Ahz-ab*), but it is clear that the first verse (In the Name of Allah) was also deleted from Sura 9, *At-Tauba* (Repentance). Al-Suyuti, a respected Muslim scholar, confirmed that more than 100 verses were deleted from that Sura.[276] He states that Ibn Malek said many verses were deleted from Sura *At-Tauba*, including 'in the name of...' and it was confirmed that it used to be equal to the number of the verses in Sura 2 (*Al-Baqara*),[277] but now the number of its verses is only 157. Where did all those verses go?

Al-Suyuti confirms something equally serious:

> "The Qur'an copy of Ibn Mas'oud contained two suras, i.e., Sura *Al-Haqd* (Ill-will), and Sura *Al-Khal'a* (Undressing); and they were placed in order after the Sura *Al-'Asr* (The Dusk).[278]

275) *The Shiite and the Correction* by Mousa Al-Mousawi, p. 131.
276) See *Al-Ittiqan* by Al-Suyuti, Vol. 1, p. 184.
277) Sura *Al-Baqara* (the Cow) has 286 verses.
278) Sura 103, *Al-'Asr* (Time [Through the Ages])

Furthermore, the Qur'an copy of Ibn Mas'oud did not contain Sura *Al-Hamd* (Praise), neither did it have Sura *Al-Mi'awathzatayn* (the two verses on seeking refuge in Allah). Those two suras were found also in the Qur'an copy of Ibn Ka'b. Ali bin Abu Talib and Umar bin Al-Kattab also used to recite those two suras."[279]

Where did those suras go? How did they disappear from the Qur'an copy of 'Uthman, which is the Qur'an read in Muslim Sunni circles today, but is different from that of the Shiites? The Sunni Qur'an has 114 suras while the Shiite Qur'an has 115, which had Sura *Al-Wilaya* (Succession) added to the Qur'an.[280]

Compilation of the Qur'an

During his lifetime, Muhammad could not gather in one book the scattered verses of what he called the Qur'an. However, Abu Bakr, his successor, started the job *fifteen years after* the death of Muhammad. After the job fell to Zayd bin Thabit, he stated:

"Ali Ibn Abu Talib came to me, asking me to pursue the Qur'an and gather it together. By Allah, if they delegated to me to move mountains, it would not have been heavier on me than doing what I was asked to do."[281]

What difficulties caused Zayd so much distress?[282] Why did he make that statement when he had the full confidence

---

279) See *Al-Ittiqan* by Al-Suyuti, Vol. 1, p. 158.
280) See Chapter 4, Footnote 20.
281) *The History of (Muslim) Legislation* by Dr. Shalabi, pp. 37-38 and the *Hadith* of Sahih Bukhari, Vol. 6, Book 60, #201.
282) For one of Zaid's difficulties, see the *Hadith* of Sahih Bukhari, Vol. 6, Book 60, #307 and Book 61, #511.

of the first and the second Caliphs? The answer lies in the
fact that he knew the Qur'an was a collection of haphazardly
scattered verses, memorized by different men.[283] Some were
alive, but many more men who memorized the Qur'anic
verses had already been killed during the raids and battles
that took place against those considered to be backsliders
from Islam.[284] Moreover, the difficult job was to find a con-
sensus among the reciters of the Qur'an regarding its word-
ing (since many words had completely different meanings,
depending on the diacritical marks). It magnified the diffi-
culty, deciding which Arabic word was which.[285]

The following assurance was made by Muhammad, that
there were four men who had good knowledge of the Qur'an.
It was recorded by Al-Bukhari:

> "Take the Qur'an from four men. They are, Ibn
> Mas'oud, bin Ka'b, Ali bin Abu Talib, and Ibn Ab-
> bas."[286]

In this statement, Muhammad did not mention Zayd.
Why then did not the first two successors of Muhammad
choose one of those four to collect the Qur'an?

Furthermore, Ibn Mas'oud confirmed that the Sura of
Praise and Sura *Al-mu'wazatein* were never a part of the
Qur'an. Al-Suyuti confirmed this in his book, *Al-Ittiqan*,
where he mentioned that 'Uthman ordered that all copies

---

283) According to the *Hadith* of Sahih Bukhari, Vol. 6, Book 60, #446,
they couldn't even agree which Sura was revealed *first* (Sura 74 *Al-
Mudathir* [the Clothed One] vs. Sura 96 *Al-Alaq* [the Clot])!
284) See the *Hadith* of Sahih Bukhari, Vol. 6, Book 61, #509.
285) In case of disagreement, the Quraish dialect and meaning was
chosen, said to be the tongue in which the Qur'an was revealed. See the
Hadith of Sahih Bukhari, Vol. 6, Book 61, #510.
286) Compare these *Ahadith* in Sahih Bukhari, Vol. 5, Book 57, #103-
105; Book 58, #150; Vol. 6, Book 61, #521, 525 & 526.

of the Qur'an be burnt – including the copy of Ali and Ibn Mas'oud.[287]

As a result of that order, a vicious war was fought between Muslims, with many victims killed. Among them was 'Uthman – one of the "preachers of Paradise" and "the man with two lights," the third successor of Muhammad. 'Uthman was slain at the hands of Muhammad bin Abu Bakr and Ammar bin Yasir (another "preacher of Paradise"). Just wondering, but according to Muhammad's teaching, where did those two preachers of Paradise go after their death, to Paradise or to hell? But that is not our concern at this time. Our concern is the fact that 'Uthman's copy of the Qur'an – the Qur'an of the majority of Muslims today – was *rejected* by a majority of Muslims in the early history of Islam! We have several questions for which we seek answers:

• Why didn't Muhammad compile the Qur'an in his life?

• Why didn't Muhammad's god or "Gabriel" command him to collect it before he died?

• Couldn't Allah guard his words (if those *were* his words) from being lost or altered?

• Couldn't Allah prevent the spilling of the blood of 'Uthman and thousands of other Muslims who differed on which were Allah's words?

Muhammad Bin Abu Bakr accused 'Uthman, as he was killing him, "You have changed Allah's book!" Therefore, Bin Abu Bakr himself – and a multitude of Muslims – said with certainty that the Qur'an has been altered. In all that mess, ask yourself: Was there really a "Gabriel" who brought down those verses? Studying all the facts that surround the Qur'an

---

287) A copy of the Qur'an belonging to one of the four men to whom Muhammad *entrusted* the Qur'an!

and its history, it seems clear that there had never been a "Gabriel," nor a god that sent down anything to Muhammad. Here was a man who claimed to be a prophet who used his god for his own purposes and to fulfill his own desires, personal and public. One Sura says:

> "Those who shout out to thee from without the inner apartments — most of them lack understanding."[288]

Al-Baydawi interpreted this:

> "What was intended by this verse were the houses of Muhammad where he used to sleep with his wives, which were considered as his secluded retreat with his wives."[289]

What a god Muhammad had, who had no concern except Muhammad and his wives. For this, his god commanded Muslims to leave Muhammad and his wives alone. O Muslims of this earth, do you really believe that God would stoop to that level? Do you believe that "Gabriel" would carry down to Muhammad verses reprimanding the Muslims who upset Muhammad's mood? Did the early Muslims think so?

A thought-provoking question. Early Muslims could not stand up to Muhammad and his god because they were afraid of being accused of backsliding away from Islam and sentenced to death for their objection. But what is the excuse of Muslims who now live in free countries?

The Hajj to Mecca

Among the five pillars of Islam is the *hajj* – the pilgrimage to Mecca, which is the duty of every financially able Muslim. The hajj was a practice of the pagans of the Arabian

---

288) Sura *Al-Hujurat* (the Chambers) 49:4.
289) *Al-Baydawi*, p. 638.

Peninsula for many centuries before Islam. It was a heathen ritual that Muhammad himself observed before he started his mission. Imam Mahmud Shaltut said:

> "Even after the conquest of Mecca, in the year 9 of the Hijra, the heathen rituals of the hajj to Mecca continued as before, with nothing changed, except that after that year, he made the hajj only for Muslims, and that the unbelievers of Mecca would either have to accept Islam or die."[290]

The walk between As-Safa and Al-Marwah was a heathen ritual,[291] as was the kissing of the black stone, the Ka'aba. Al-Bukhari wrote:

> "An Arab said to Anas bin Malik: 'Did you refuse to walk between As-Safa and Al-Marwah?' He answered, 'Yes, because it was one of the rituals of the heathen epoch, but Allah adopted it as a law of his.'"

Muslim's Sahih also confirmed what Bukhari wrote, but added the following statement by Ibn Abbas:

> "During the heathen epoch (known as *Al-Jahilya*), demons used to roam during the whole night between those two mountains."[292]

Regarding kissing the black stone, Umar Ibn al-Khattab said:

---

290) *Islam, a Doctrine and a Legislation*, by Sheikh Mahmud Shaltut (1893-1963), pp. 113-114.
291) *As-Safa* and *Al-Marwah* are two hills of Mecca. For the myth of Hagar running between the hills, see the *Hadith* of Sahih Bukhari, Vol. 4, Book 55, #584. Also the story of Abraham in Chapter 10 of this book.
292) See the *Hadith* of Sahih Bukhari, Vol. 2, Book 26, #706 & 710; Vol. 3, Book 27, #18; Vol. 6, Book 60, #22-23 & 38 and the *Hadith* of Sahih Muslim, Book 7, Chapter 41 "Sa'i between Al-Safa and Al-Marwa Is an Essential Rite of Hajj and Hajj Is Not Complete Without It," #2923-2928.

"By Allah, had I not seen the Messenger of Allah kissing it, I would not have kissed it."

It was well known that the Arabs of the heathen epoch used to come to Mecca for pilgrimage and kiss that stone.

The Qur'an turned the facts upside down or ignored them in several cases, even though it sometimes based itself on the Bible. But it is clear that the Qur'an did not quote the Bible, either literally or figuratively. So the stories that were recorded in it were distorted and twisted, such as the stories of Joseph, Job, Jonah, Moses, Pharaoh, Haman and others.

6

Christ vs. Muhammad

In this chapter, we will prove the deity of Christ from the Qur'an and the Statements of Muhammad, called *Al-Hadith* (Tradition). We will also discuss Christ's birth, life and crucifixion. And we will compare the life of Muhammad, the Muslim prophet, with the life of Christ.

The Annunciation and Christ's Birth
"And the Word was made flesh, and dwelt among us, and we beheld his glory, the glory as of the only begotten of the Father, full of grace and truth." Then, John the Baptist testified about Jesus, saying: "This was he of whom I spake, He that cometh after me is preferred before me, for he was before me. And of his fullness have all we received, and grace for grace."[293]

The Gospel of John, chapter 1:14, gives the meaning of the birth of Christ. John says, "He that cometh after me... for he was before me." How could Christ have come *before* John the Baptist if Christ was born about six months *after*

---

293) John 1:15-16.

John? The concept is clear. John was speaking of the eternality of Christ, for He was, is and will be.

John continued, "And of his fullness all we received." Why would John say "we," including the whole world? Because Jesus Christ is not a prophet or a messenger but the Almighty God, who became incarnate in the person of Jesus Christ. Thus we all could receive of His fullness.

The Gospel of Luke and the Qur'an also speak of the birth of Christ. Luke says:

> "And in the sixth month the angel Gabriel was sent from God unto a city of Galilee named Nazareth, to a virgin espoused to a man whose name was Joseph, of the house of David; and the virgin's name was Mary. And the angel came in unto her, and said, Hail, thou that art highly favoured, the Lord is with thee: blessed art thou among women. And when Mary saw him, she was troubled at his saying, and cast in her mind what manner of salutation this should be. And the angel said unto her, Fear not, Mary: for thou hast found favour with God. And, behold, thou shalt conceive in thy womb, and bring forth a son, and shalt call his name Jesus. He shall be great, and shall be called the Son of the Highest: and the Lord God shall give unto him the throne of his father David. And he shall reign over the house of Jacob for ever, and of his kingdom there shall be no end."[294]

Thus came Gabriel, the angel of peace, to Mary, and began his mission by saying, "Peace be unto thee."[295] Here, we did

---

294) Luke 1:26-33.
295) This is the meaning of "hail." See Albert Barnes' *Notes on the Bible* and Adam Clarke's *Commentary on the Bible* at this verse.

not see Mary stricken with terror to the point of passing out or foaming at the mouth, or feeling she was being choked to death. Nor did she say that she thought whatever appeared to her was death or devils, as Muhammad described his "Gabriel." On the contrary, when Gabriel appeared to Mary, she was filled with peace, security, assurance, joy and the Holy Ghost!

In comparing this Annunciation story in Luke 1 with the story found in the Qur'an, Sura 19 (*Maryam*), notice that Muhammad attempted to write in his Qur'an what was recorded in Luke. The angel brought to her the good news... But let us see how the Qur'an deviated and fabricated events as Muhammad erroneously attempted to recite the story:

> "Relate (remember) in the Book [the Gospel] (the story of) Mary, when she withdrew from her family to a place in the East. She placed a screen (to screen herself) from them; then We sent her our angel and he appeared before her as a man in all respects. She said: 'I seek refuge from thee to ((Allah)) Most Gracious: (come not near) if thou dost fear Allah. He said: 'Nay, I am only a messenger from thy Lord, (to announce) to thee the gift of a holy son.' She said: 'How shall I have a son, seeing that no man has touched me, and I am not unchaste?' He said: 'So (it will be): thy Lord saith, "That is easy for me: and (We wish) to appoint him as a Sign unto men and a Mercy from us." It is a matter (so) decreed.' So she conceived him, and she retired with him to a remote place. And the pains of childbirth drove her to the trunk of a palm-tree: she cried (in her anguish): 'Ah! Would that I had died before this! Would that I had been a thing forgotten and out of sight.' But

(a voice) cried to her from beneath the (palm tree): 'Grieve not! For thy Lord hath provided a rivulet beneath thee; and shake towards thyself the trunk of the palm-tree: it will let fall fresh ripe dates upon thee. So eat and drink and cool (thine) eye. And if thou dost see any man, say, "I have vowed a fast to ((Allah)) Most Gracious, to fast; and this day will I enter into no talk with any human being.""296

Clearly, what was recorded in the Qur'an is a false, illogical fabrication. The additions to the story were distortions of the real story of Christ's birth written in the Gospel of Luke. In the Qur'an the story totally differs, depicting Mary as a scared young lady, but does not tell why. Then it says she sought a secluded place away from her family, but does not say why she was afraid of her family – especially since there was nothing to be afraid of. She was not yet pregnant. The Qur'an's account, to that point, is illogical and meaningless, because the Qur'an says the angel came to her before she became pregnant, to reassure her and fill her with the Holy Spirit of God. There was no reason for her fear.

Further, the Qur'an says that Mary ran away from her hometown to a wilderness, where she gave birth. The fact is that Mary did not run away at all, for all the people of Nazareth knew she was married to Joseph, and they could see that she was with child. Her arrival in Bethlehem was not because she was running away, but as the Bible explains:

"... it came to pass in those days, that there went out a decree from Caesar Augustus, that all the world should be taxed. And this taxing was first made, when Cyrenius was governor of Syria. And all went to be taxed, every one into his own city. And Joseph also

296) Sura *Maryam* (Mary), 19:16-26.

went up from Galilee, out of the city of Nazareth, into Judea, unto the city of David, which is called Bethlehem, because he was of the house and lineage of David; to be taxed with Mary his espoused wife, being great with child. And so, it was that, while they were there, the days were accomplished that she should be delivered. And she brought forth her firstborn son, and she wrapped him in swaddling clothes, and laid him in a manger; because there was no room for them in the inn."[297]

The Bible does not say she was afraid, or that she ran away, or that she screened herself from her family, or that she went to some wilderness. Rather, she went with her espoused husband to be registered in the city of David, in obedience to the law of Caesar, where she gave birth to Jesus.

Another deviation from the true story is the Qur'an's claim that Mary gave birth to the child near the trunk of a palm-tree, as told in the Sura of Mary 19:23:

"And the pain of childbirth drove her to the trunk of a palm-tree: she cried, Ah! Would that I had died before this! Would that I had been a thing forgotten and out of sight."

(A very vivid imagination, but very false). We have to ask: Why did she wish death on herself while she was carrying in her womb the Blessed One, whose birth the angels had great joy in announcing:

"… Fear not: for, behold, *I bring you good tidings of great joy*, which shall be to all people; for unto you is born this day, in the city of David, a Saviour, which is Christ the Lord?"[298]

---

297) Luke 2:1-7.
298) Luke 2:10-11.

How could a woman who was carrying in her womb Christ the Lord say, as the Qur'an put it:

"Ah! Would that I had died before this, would that I had been a thing forgotten and out of sight?"

Usually, a woman with a natural child, despite the birth pains, is happy and proud to give birth to a regular child, let alone a heavenly Child. How could that dreadful thing the Qur'an mentions happen when the archangel assured her, "Peace be unto you," and the Holy Spirit filled her? The distortions in the Qur'an are many and clearly illogical.

How could any Muslim say that the Qur'an is more truthful than the Gospel, knowing that the Qur'an came about 600 years *after* the writing of the Gospel, and knowing that *the Qur'an itself* carried a forthright testimony that the Gospel is the Book of God? Since it is the Book of God by the testimony of the Qur'an, then God should make sure that the Gospel is protected from any change. This will be discussed in Chapter 9.

Christ is mentioned by name 25 times in its Suras, while Muhammad's name is mentioned three times. In all those mentions, the Qur'an gives Christ distinctives it did not give to any other prophet, as though it was giving Jesus the attributes of God; then it turns around and contradicts itself. The Qur'an tells a strange story in Sura *Maryam* 19:29-30:

"But she pointed to the babe. They said, 'How can we talk to one who is a child in the cradle?' He (the babe who was in the cradle) said, 'I am indeed a servant of Allah; He hath given me revelation and made me a prophet.'"

Here, an infant who was a few hours old is speaking and answering the charges of people, defending his mother.

Here baby Jesus spoke after some people accused her of a shameful act, as the Qur'an mentions:

> "At length she brought the babe to her people, carrying him. They said, 'O Mary! Truly an amazing thing hast thou brought; O sister of Aaron, thy father was not a man of evil, nor thy mother a woman unchaste.'"[299]

According to the Qur'an, Mary's family expressed their disapproval of what happened to her. But the Bible tells us a totally different story, *the true story*:

> "Now, the birth of Jesus Christ was on this wise: When as his mother Mary was espoused to Joseph, before they came together, she was found with child of the Holy Ghost. Then Joseph her husband, being a just man, and not willing to make her a publick example, was minded to put her away privily (secretly). But while he thought on these things, behold, the angel of the Lord appeared unto him in a dream, saying, Joseph, thou son of David, fear not to take unto thee Mary thy wife: for that which is conceived in her is of the Holy Ghost."[300]

Mary was evidently a believing woman, who lived her faith, and was well known for her purity among her relatives and friends. The Bible describes her husband, Joseph, the carpenter, as a righteous man. He decided to divorce her secretly so no one would know about her situation. But the angel of the Lord came down and convinced him not to divorce her. The story continued in its normal course. No blame, no criticism, no condemnation. The Qur'an introduced a totally new story that is totally twisted and fabricated.

---

299) Sura *Maryam* 19:27-28.
300) Matthew 1:18-20.

Christ should not be compared to any prophet, let alone Muhammad. But we will do it to show the truth that everyone is entitled to know.

The Birth of Muhammad Comparison

The Sheikh of Islam, Muhammad bin Abd Al-Wahab, said that there is no contention about the place of Muhammad's birth, Mecca, or the year of his birth, the year of the elephant.[301] But by saying there is no contention, he implies that there is some doubt; and the matter is subject to assumption and not certainty. Further, Al-Wahab tells us that scholars differ on whether Abd Allah died before or after Muhammad's birth.[302] Most probably he died before Muhammad's birth.

Then, there was a contention concerning his mother's death. Some claim that she died between Mecca and Medina while she was on her way to visit his uncles in Medina before he was six years old. (It should be noted that nothing was written in the Qur'an about the birth of Muhammad.)

In contrast, not only the details of the birth of Christ were recorded, but also the prophecies that detailed his birth over 600 years *before* His birth, by Isaiah and other prophets.[303] Then the Gospel continued to tell us about the amazing story of Christ's birth:

> "Now when Jesus was born in Bethlehem of Judea in the days of Herod the king, behold there came wise men from the east to Jerusalem, saying, Where is he that is born King of Jews? For we have seen his star in the east, and are come to worship him."[304]

301) *The Life of the Prophet* by Muhammad bin Abd Al-Wahab, p. 30.
302) See *The Life of the Prophet*, p. 32
303) For instance, see Isaiah 7:14; 9:6-7; and Micah 5:2.
304) Matthew 2:1-2.

Matthew said that on the day the wise men came to see the newborn Christ, the whole world glowed with bright lights, and the skies shook on the day of His crucifixion.[305]

Christ did not come to this world by surprise or accident. Extensive prophetic preparations were made for his coming, thousands of years before he came, through prophets such as Abraham, Jacob, Moses and others. Isaiah, one of the greatest prophets, who lived in the eighth century before Christ, predicted the birth of Christ and the manner of that birth:

"Therefore, the Lord himself shall give you a sign; behold, a virgin shall conceive, and bear a son, and shall call his name Immanuel" (meaning God with us).[306]

Then Isaiah the prophet continued to identify this miraculous person who was to be born, quoting Almighty God:

"For unto us a child is born, unto us a son is given, and the government shall be upon his shoulder: and his name shall be called Wonderful, Counsellor, the Mighty God, the everlasting Father, the Prince of Peace."[307]

Not only was his birth prophesied, but also his life, ministry and death. Isaiah was again given the revelation in the eighth century before Christ, describing Christ crucifixion:

"Surely he hath borne our griefs, and carried our sorrows: yet we did esteem him stricken, smitten of God and afflicted. But he was wounded for our transgressions, he was bruised for our iniquities: the chastisement of our peace was upon him, and with his stripes we were healed."[308]

---

305) See Matthew 2:2, 9-10; 27:51 & 54.
306) Isaiah 7:14.
307) Isaiah 9:6.
308) Isaiah 53:4-5.

Isaiah continued to describe His going to the cross to die for our sins:

> "And the Lord hath laid on him the iniquity of us all. He was oppressed, and he was afflicted, yet he opened not his mouth: he is brought as a lamb to the slaughter, and as a sheep before his shearers is dumb, so he openeth not his mouth."[309]

The two volumes from before Muhammad that spoke of Christ's birth were acknowledged by him, namely the "Torah" and the "Gospel" (The Old and the New Testaments). The Torah (the Old Testament) spoke about every phase of Christ's life, including His birth, birthplace, forerunner, ministry, miracles, disciples, trial, crucifixion, burial and glorious resurrection.

Muslims blame Christians for not acknowledging the Qur'an or the prophethood of Muhammad, even though Muhammad and his Qur'an recognize and endorse Christ and all the prophets who came before him. Frankly, the Qur'an acknowledges all those truths because he could not deny the historical facts that took place more than 600 years earlier. Within that short period of the history of the nations between Christ and Muhammad, Christianity spread throughout all corners of the known world. It did this without the sword and marching armies to convince people by force and coercion of the message of Christ.

Those disciples, who were sent into the world as sheep into the midst of wolves,[310] could win the world with Christ's love and compassion. Even when the sword seemed to be needed, when Peter attempted to use his sword to defend his Master, Christ reprimanded him:

---

309) Isaiah 53:6-7.
310) See Matthew 10:16.

"Put up thy sword into the sheath: the cup which my Father hath given me, shall I not drink it?"[311]

Sin in the Life of the Prophets

Muhammad confessed that he was no more than just a human. The Qur'an clearly proves that fact:

"Say, I am but a man like yourselves."[312]

The Qur'an speaks of Muhammad's past sins as well as those that followed during his lifetime. In other words, Muhammad committed a multitude of sins, and some of those sins would not possibly be committed by ordinary men. I am not trying to criticize or attack the person of Muhammad, but rather clarifying a fact I wish with all my heart did not exist. But even his Qur'an describes Muhammad as a sinner, and his god commands him to ask forgiveness of his sins and the sins of his followers:

"… and ask forgiveness for thy fault [guilt], and for the men and the women who believe…."[313]

In contrast, the Bible assures us that the Lord Jesus Christ was *not* a regular human, but a perfect man who lived and died without committing any sin. For this reason, He could challenge the world: "Which of you convinceth (convicts) me of sin?"[314] Then, the Lord Jesus affirms by his great and mighty works and miracles that it was God the Father who had sent Him to the world:

"Say ye of him, whom the Father hath sanctified, and sent into the world, Thou blasphemest, because I said, I am the Son of God?"[315]

---

311) John 18:11.
312) Sura *Al-Kahf* (the Cave) 18:110.
313) Sura *Muhammad* 47:19.
314) John 8:46.
315) John 10:36.

This is Jesus, the Son of God. This does not mean that God gave birth to His Son, or that God married a woman, who gave Jesus birth. God forbid! God and Christ the Son of God is not by birth. The Son emanated from the Father.

The Intercession of Muhammad

The Bible forthrightly tells us that Jesus Christ is the only intercessor and the only mediator between men and God:

> "For there is One God and One Mediator between God and men, the man (who died for us on the cross) Christ Jesus."[316]

John continued comforting the brethren:

> "My little children, these things write I unto you, that ye sin not. And if any man sin, we have an advocate with the Father, Jesus Christ the righteous."[317]

On the other hand, many Muslims believe that Muhammad can be their intercessor and mediator before God. But he cannot mediate for himself, much less for others. In other words, the Qur'an teaches that Muhammad cannot, under any circumstances, be a mediator or intercessor:

> "Whether thou ask for their forgiveness, or not, (their sin is unforgivable): if thou ask seventy times for their forgiveness, Allah will not forgive them."[318]

Muhammad's actions prove it was impossible for him to be a prophet of God. Here are many more reasons:

1. Muhammad committed the sin of adultery when he married Zainab without witnesses or a guardian. He also committed many other incidents of adultery.

2. Muhammad committed the crime of killing, and urging

316) 1 Timothy 2:5.
317) 1 John 2:1.
318) Sura *At-Tauba* (Repentance) 9:80.

others to kill, raid, rob and spill innocent blood. Muhammad bin Abd Al-Wahab wrote:

> "When he (Muhammad) was in Al-Safra area, he divided the spoils, and killed Al-Nadr bin Al-Harith. Then, when he went down to Irq Al-Zabia he killed Aqaba bin Abi Mu'ayyet."[319]

Muhammad seemed to kill men for the joy of killing.

4. The best trade Muhammad had was buying and selling slaves. Ibn Qayyim Al-Jawziyya said:

> "The purchasing of slaves by Muhammad was much more that his selling slaves."[320]

Al-Halabi described an incident involving Muhammad:

> "One day, Muhammad went to the (slavery) market where he found Zaher, a friend of his. He embraced him from the back, and covered his eyes. Zaher asked, Who is this? Muhammad replied, I am the slave trader."[321]

Fathi Radwan wrote:

> "The fame of Muhammad was to buy and sell slaves."[322]

5. Muhammad robbed and pillaged caravans as they traveled between Mecca and Damascus. In the process, he killed some men and took others captive and enslaved the women and the children.

6. He was stricken by pride and arrogance. He behaved as though he were the king of kings. He had a servant whose sole job was to take care of his shoes and put them on his

---

319) *The Brief of the Life of the Prophet* by Muhammad bin Abd Al-Wahab, p. 92.
320) *Zad Al-Ma'ad* by Ibn Qayyim Al-Jawziyya, Vol. I, p. 160.
321) *Al-Sira Al-Halabia* by Al-Halabi, Vol. III, p. 441.
322) *The Greatest Revolutionary* by Fathi Radwan, p. 140.

feet. Ibn Kathir said that Ibn Malek served the Messenger for ten years as his shoe care-taker.[323] No real prophet of God, before or after him, demonstrated such arrogance.

Other known servants were Ibn Sharik, Asma' bin Haritha, Balal bin Riyah, Rabi'a bin Ka'b. Abd Allah bin Mas'oud used to carry his shoes, and Al-Moughira bin Sha'bia was his bodyguard, even though he was well known for his womanizing, marrying four women at a time, then divorcing them to marry the next four. (Al-Hassan bin Ali, Muhammad's grandson, used to follow the same ritual as Mas'oud in marriage.) Al-Halabi confirms this:

> "Ibn Mas'oud was specialized in carrying the shoes of the Messenger (Muhammad). If he got up to walk, he would put the shoes on the prophet's feet; and when he sat down, Ibn Mas'oud would take off the shoes and carry them until he (Muhammad) got up."[324]

How do we compare Muhammad and his arrogance with Christ, who washed the feet of His disciples?

7. Muhammad is portrayed by Muslims as the poor prophet. But he was far from poor. Al-Halabi describes Muhammad's assets and properties after he took over Arabia:

> "He owned seven horses, and some said that he owned fifteen or twenty Arabian horses, six mules, two donkeys, three camels ready to be ridden, one hundred sheep, and thirty bond-maids. As for the gold and the silver that he owned, there is no count. One of his companions asked him, 'Why do you wipe the horse with your garment?' He answered, 'Who knows, maybe "Gabriel" commanded me to do so.'"[325]

---

323) *The Beginning and the End* by Ibn Kathir, Vol. V, p. 331.

324) *Al-Sira Al-Halabia* by Al-Halabi, Vol. III, p. 420.

325) *Al-Sira Al-Halabia* by Al-Halabi, Vol. III, p. 429.

Poor "Gabriel" was not spared even from that trivial matter. Whenever someone objected to Muhammad's behavior, some companion would say, "Did not one verse come down to justify that behavior?" Or "Did not 'Gabriel' command him to do that?" Were his companions joking?

Could it be possible for Muhammad to be a prophet of God? I personally doubt it, even if we assume that Jesus is just a prophet and not God, as Muslims say. Please note the great differences in the actions and behaviors of the two men. Christ is incomparable. He has no equal!

Muhammad Under the Power of Satan

It was Muhammad himself who distinguished Christ from all humans. He was quoted by Al-Bushari:

> "Satan pokes with his finger the side of every human at birth, except Jesus, the son of Mary, when he went to poke him, he poked the curtain."[326]

Why could Satan not poke Jesus? The answer is in the words of Christ Himself:

> "Hereafter I will not talk much with you; for the prince of this world (Satan) cometh, and hath nothing in me."[327]

When Satan came to tempt Jesus, the Lord commanded him to depart: "Get thee hence Satan."[328] Only Christ could give Satan orders because He is the Almighty God, and Satan has no choice but to obey the Lord Jesus Christ.

However, Satan has power over all sinful men. The Qur'an tells us clearly that Satan had power over Muhammad:

326) See also the *Hadith* of Sahih Bukhari, Vol. 4, Book 54, #506; Book 55, #641; Vol. 6, Book 60, #71; and the *Hadith* of Sahih Muslim, Book 30, #5837-5839; and Book 33, #6429.
327) John 14:30.
328) Matthew 4:10.

"Say I seek refuge from the mischief of those who practice secret arts."[329]

The Qur'an further proves Satan's power over Muhammad:

"If a suggestion from Satan assail thy (mind)...."[330]

Furthermore, Muhammad claimed that some Jew put an evil spell on him. How could a prophet of God be forced under an evil spell, when he himself should have had the power to cast out devils? Some Muslim scholars try to deny that Muhammad was put under an evil spell, even though most Muslim historians acknowledge that appalling fact. The greatest contemporary Muslim scholars agree that Muhammad had been put under an evil spell. As-Suhaili wrote:

"Lubaid bin Al-A'sam of the clan of Zuraiq put the spell on Muhammad. This matter was made public and well known among the people and confirmed by all the scholars that wrote the Hadith (sayings of Muhammad). Mo'ammar quoted Al-Zuheiri saying that the Prophet was under the evil spell for one year. He used to imagine that he did something when he did not do anything. The knots of the spell were eleven knots, and Zainab the Jewess helped Lubaid bin Al-A'sam to accomplish that."[331]

Al-Bukhari wrote,[332] giving a complete explanation as to what happened to...

"the Master of all prophets and messengers, Muhammad bin Abd Allah, and how he was placed under an evil spell by Lubaid with the help of his own

---

329) Sura *Al-Falaq* (the Daybreak) 113:1, 4.

330) Sura *Al-A'raf* (the Heights) 7:200.

331) *Rawd Al-Unuf* by As-Suhaili, Vol. II, pp. 290-291.

332) This is confirmed by no less than Aisha herself! See the *Hadith* of Sahih Bukhari, Vol. 4, Book 54, #490; and Vol. 8, Book 73, #89.

daughters, who took some of Muhammad's hair and his comb, which they buried in the well of Zi Arwan, which was in one of the city's gardens."

Those who want to be sure of the story that Muhammad, Allah's messenger, was placed under the power of Satan by an evil spell, may read many Islamic references confirming this.[333] Sheikh Muhammad Mutawalli Al-Sha'rawi wrote:

"This matter, that is, the placing of the Messenger of Allah under an evil spell, is recorded in Al-Bukhari's Sahih, and it is definitely accepted as a fact, where he imagined (hallucinated) that he was doing something when he did not do it."[334]

Muslim scholars should note that the Jews succeeded in placing Muhammad under an evil spell when he was sixty years old, twenty years *after* claiming that he became a prophet of Allah. That is when Aisha said that he used to sleep with his wives, and then forget that he slept with them.[335]

Muhammad, claiming to be a prophet, a messenger of God, "the master of all messengers, and the seal of all the prophets," was placed under an evil spell to the extent that he could not differentiate between things for one whole year! Had it not been for Lubaid bin Al-A'sam, who was paid a huge amount of money to take the evil spells off Muhammad, he would have remained in the shackles of those evil

---

333) See *Al-Sira Al-Halabia* by Al-Halabi, Vol. III, p. 501; *The Jurisprudence of the Life of Muhammad*, by Dr. Al-Bouti, a great Azhar University professor, p. 358; *Al-Rawd Al-Aaniq* by As-Suhaili, Vol. 2, pp. 290-291; *Jawami' Al-Sira* by Ibn Hazm, p. 35; *Al-Jalalayn* by Jalal & Jalal, p. 522; *The Causes of Descendancy* by Al-Suyuti, p. 310; *The Commentary of Al-Baydawi*, p. 518; and *Zad Al-Ma'ad* by Ibn Qayyim Al-Jawziyya, Vol. V, pp. 62-63.

334) *You Ask and Islam Answers* by Mutawalli Al-Sha'rawi, Vol. II, p. 406.

335) See Footnote 40 above.

spells. After Lubaid freed him from the spell, Muhammad was asked, "Were you really under the spell." He answered, "Yes, but my lord freed me of the spell, and he sent down upon me the two suras known in Arabic as *Al-Mi'wazthatayn* (asking for refuge in Allah).

Is it possible that Muhammad was insane? How could the Muslim general public believe such a travesty, that this man was a prophet of the Almighty God? Read the Qur'an, not anything else. Will you find that any of the twenty-four prophets mentioned in the Qur'an were placed under an evil spell, or were chained under the total control of Satan, like Muhammad was? *No one else but Muhammad.*

After all that, my Muslim people still say that Muhammad is "the seal of the prophets and the master of all messengers!" What prophets? Which messengers? If the master of all messengers was put under an evil spell and the control of Satan, and the seal of the prophets had such atrocious behavior, how bad must the other prophets be? I ask this question of my Muslim people so they may realize the difference between a real prophet and the false claims of a false prophet.

Note: real prophets had a much higher standard of morals and holiness than Muhammad.

In another comparison, Christ said:

> "You have heard that it hath been said, An eye for an eye and a tooth for a tooth. But I say unto you, That ye resist not evil, but whosoever shall smite thee on thy right cheek, turn to him the other also."[336]

But the Prophet of Islam says:

> "I am commanded to fight people until they say, No

---

336) Matthew 5:39.

god but Allah. If they said it, their blood and their properties would be spared."[337]

He continued in Sura *At-Tauba*:

"O Prophet! Strive hard against the unbelievers and the Hypocrites, and be firm (cruel) against them."[338]

Jesus did greater miracles than anyone before or after Him. The eyewitnesses to His miracles proclaimed that He was matchless. The Bible says the people were...

"beyond measure astonished, saying, He hath done all things well, he makes both the deaf to hear, and the dumb to speak."[339]

In contrast, Muhammad silenced people in the cruelest ways. Fatima Umm Qirfa was remembered by the way Muhammad killed her in her old age. He tied her hands and legs to two opposing camels and made them gallop in opposite ways so the woman was cut in half.[340]

Jesus restored sight to the blind and planted joy and happiness in people's hearts. In contrast, Muhammad commanded his people to kill, raid, rob and pluck out the eyes of others in the most cruel ways. Sheikh Al-Khudri wrote:

"Some Arabians killed, while in violent confrontation, one of the companions of Muhammad. Muhammad sent some of his men to arrest them and to bring them to him. When they were brought before him, he ordered their hands and then their legs be cut off, after that, he ordered that their eyes be (hot)

---

337) See Chapter 4, Footnote #66 for references.
338) Sura *At-Tauba* (Repentance) 9:73.
339) Mark 7:37.
340) See *Rawd Al-Unuf* by As-Suhaili, Vol. 4, pp. 237-252; *The Complete in History* by Ibn Al-Athir, Vol. II, p. 142; *Al-Sira Al-Halabia* by Al-Halabi, Vol. III, p. 181; and other Muslim writers.

nailed. Then they were thrown in a ditch (as a mass grave), where they were left to die."[341]

This story was also recorded in the *Hadith* of Sahih Bukhari[342] and in many books by Muslim scholars. Could a man with such cruelty be the prophet of mercy?

The god of Muhammad, in accordance with the Qur'an, is a god of cruelty and deception, as was listed in the good names of Allah list. The Qur'an describes Allah:

"The deceiver, and Allah also deceived them."

"You deceive, but Allah is the best of all deceivers."

Could the real God be such a god with such a description?[343] Or such cruelty?

Is Allah holy, just, loving and the One who forgives all our sins by the intercession of Jesus Christ? Far be it from us that our God should be the same god as Muhammad's!

I apologize to all Christians for comparing Christ with Muhammad and his morals; for comparing the Creator, the King of Peace, with a man who violated the laws of life and those of God, making an alliance with the sword to fulfill his own lusts, claiming he was a prophet.

---

341) *The Light of Certainty* (Nur Al-Yaqin) by Al-Khudri, 24th edition, pp. 184-185.

342) See Chapter 4, Footnote #37.

343) For instance, see Suras *An-Nisa'* (the Women) 4:88; *Al-An'am* (the Cattle) 6:39; *Ar-Ra'd* (the Thunder) 13:27; *Ibrahim* 14:4; *An-Nahl* (the Bee) 16:93; *Al-Mu'min* (the Forgiving One) 40:34; and *Al-Mudathir* (the Clothed One) 74:31.

7

Christ in The Qur'an

The Qur'an follows the life of Christ, from His birth to His death and resurrection, with hundreds of verses. Twenty-five of them mention the name "Jesus."[344]

In this chapter we will quote definite and confirmed verses, not subject to "The Annulling and the Annulled" in the Qur'an. They are "sure" verses that Muhammad did not change his mind about. They were validated by the collectors of the Qur'an, namely 'Uthman ibn 'Affan; Ali bin Abu Talib; Abd Allah bin Mas'oud; and Abi bin Ka'b; and even those verses recorded in the Qur'an that were collected by Zayd bin Thabit, in the days of Umar's and 'Uthman's Caliphates. (Ironically, bin Thabit was killed for standing up for his compilation of the Qur'an. Muhammad bin Abu Bakr stabbed him thirty times as he declared: "You have altered the Book of Allah!") The Qur'an remains as it was decided by 'Uthman until this day.

Sura *Al-Imran* affirms the truth of the Gospel and the Torah:

---

344) Also, 23 verses in the Qur'an refer to Jesus as "the son of Mary" and 11 call Him "the Messiah." (Some verses use 2 or all 3 terms.)

"It is He Who sent down to thee (step by step) in truth, the Book … and He sent down the Law (of Moses) and the Gospel (of Jesus) before this, as a guide to mankind, and He sent down the criterion (of judgment between right and wrong)."[345]

Therefore, Muhammad acknowledged that the Bible is God's Word, and his Qur'an testifies to that fact. The Qur'an tells a story about the birth of Christ, as a virgin was chosen to give Him birth:

"Behold, the angels said, O Mary! Allah hath chosen thee and purified thee — chosen thee above the women of all nations."[346]

It continues,

"Behold, the angel said, O Mary! Allah giveth thee glad tidings of a Word from Him, his name will be Christ Jesus, the son of Mary, held in honor in this world and the hereafter, and of those who are nearest to Allah. He shall speak to people in childhood (the cradle) and in maturity, and shall be of the righteous."[347]

Remember: the Qur'an tells the story of Christ, sometimes quoting Bible verses, but mostly adding to it or deleting facts from it.

1. The Qur'an records what it claims are the life and deeds of Christ.

"And appointed him an apostle to the children of Israel, (with this message), I have come to you, with

---

345) Sura *Al-Imran* (the Family of Imran) 3:3.
346) Sura *Al-Imran* (the House of Imran) 3:42. Note the Catholic doctrine of Mary being chosen "above" all women, rather than "among" them, as it says in Luke 1:28 & 42.
347) Sura *Al-Imran* 3:45-46.

a sign from your Lord, in that I create for you out of clay, as it were, the figure of a bird, and I breathe into it, and it becomes a bird,[348] by Allah's leave; and I heal those who are born blind, and the lepers, and I quicken the dead, by Allah's leave, and I declare to you what you eat, and what you store in your houses. Surely therein is a sign for you if ye did believe."[349]

This story was repeated in the Qur'an.[350] In fact, more than 25% of the verses in the Qur'an are repeated. Perhaps Muhammad and/or "Gabriel" were absent-minded, so they forgot that the verse was recited earlier. As Muhammad said, "Who does not inadvertently forget, except Allah?" That gives "Gabriel" or Muhammad an excuse for forgetting.

In the above verse, Muhammad affirmed that Christ is God and not a prophet because the attribute of creating is God's only, and God has never given that power to anyone. If God allowed humans to have it, there would be competition between God and humans. Chaos would ensue. But Christ was quoted in the Qur'an as saying:

"I create for you out of clay, as it were, the figure of a bird, and I breathe into it, and it becomes a bird."

This text clearly indicates that Christ is God, the Creator.

2. Another Qur'anic basis for affirming the deity of Christ in the above verse is the fact that Jesus raised the dead. Who can raise the dead to life, especially after they stank? When Christ raised Lazarus from the dead after four days, corruption started to affect his corpse.[351] That becomes a process of

---

348) This refers to stories in the fake "Infancy Gospel of Thomas," known as I Infancy 2:1-5.
349) Sura *Al-Imran* 3:49.
350) The story is repeated in Sura *Al-Ma'idah* (the Table) 5:110.
351) See John 11:39.

creation accompanying the process of raising the dead. All He had to do was to say "Lazarus, come forth," and he did. He is also the One who said: "Let there be ..." and it was. Is that not the attribute of God alone?

3. The Qur'an affirms that Christ had another attribute that belongs only to God. He did miracles that no one else, neither before or after Him, could do. He healed the sick, opened the eyes of the blind, the mouth of the dumb and the ears of the deaf, and He cleansed the lepers. The Bible says: "I am the Lord that healeth thee."[352] Indeed, Christ is the real healer.

A very important point should be noted here. In all the references in the Qur'an, whenever a person does something extraordinary, there is always a reference attached to it; namely, by Allah's will, as Allah wishes, by Allah's permission or leave, or by Allah's order. In the Gospels those phrases are never used because *Jesus* is the Lord who commands. He commanded Lazarus to rise from the dead, and he did. He commanded the paralyzed man to get up and walk, and he did. Christ never asked for permission because He is God Almighty. If Christ were just a prophet or a messenger and acted as though the power were His, God would have immediately stripped Him of His powers, or punished Him for not glorifying or obeying God, as He did with Herod Agrippa,[353] prophets[354] and others.[355] But Christ continued throughout His ministry to let people know that the power was solely His. For this reason, He could say:

---

352) Exodus 15:26.
353) See Acts 12:21-23.
354) For instance, see 1 Kings 13:26
355) For instance, Achan (Joshua 7), King Saul (1 Samuel 15:22-23), King Uzziah (2 Chronicles 26:16-23), etc.

"I am the bread of life: he that cometh to me shall never hunger; and he that believeth on me shall never thirst."[356]

The Qur'an says in *Al-Imran* 3:48 that Allah will teach Jesus the Book, the wisdom, the Torah and the Gospel. But the Qur'an continued to say that Jesus was able to quicken the dead and create life. Would someone who can heal, raise the dead and create life need to be taught anything about this world and eternity? Jesus is the Lord who inspired all the words that were written in the Gospels and all the books of the Old and New Testament.

Jesus confronted the Pharisees, who knew that Christ would be the son of David, but not that He would be God. Jesus asked them, if Christ is the son of David, "How then doth David in the spirit call him Lord?"[357] The Pharisees, who were the religious leaders of those days, were dumbfounded because they could see that king David, who was also a prophet, could see Jesus in the spirit of prophecy, as the Lord God Almighty. Consequently, the Lord Jesus could rightfully declare:

"I and the Father are one."[358]

He continued:

"He that hath seen me hath seen the Father."[359]

Finally, when Thomas saw the undeniable truth, he shouted: "My Lord and My God!"[360]

Paul the apostle, in the first epistle to Timothy, focusing on the fact that Jesus is God, said:

---

356) John 6:35.
357) Matthew 22:43.
358) John 10:30.
359) John 14:9.
360) John 20:28.

"And without controversy great is the mystery of godliness: God was manifest in the flesh."[361]

Then Paul describes in detail the truth about Jesus Christ:

"Who is the image of the invisible God... For by him were all things created, that are in heaven, and that are in earth, visible and invisible, whether they be thrones, or dominions, or principalities, or powers: all things were created by him, and for him: And he is before all things, and by him all things consist."[362]

If you study the attributes of Christ in the Qur'an, you will realize that the Qur'an affirms in Christ the attributes that belong only to God. When the Qur'an speaks of Christ, it does not describe Him as a prophet, because even the Qur'an cannot deny that He is God!

The Qur'an mentions 25 prophets, including Muhammad. The question here is, "Which one of all those prophets could do *any* of the miracles that Christ performed?" All those prophets together, with all their powers, could not have made one single miracle like the ones Christ did. Could Muhammad heal any sick person? *He could not even heal himself!* Muhammad could not guarantee anyone eternal life. He could not guarantee that for himself. In fact, the only thing Muhammad could guarantee was that all Muslims would go to hell:

"Not one of you but will arrive in it. This is with thy Lord a determined must."[363]

When Muhammad was asked, "Will you also arrive in Hell?" He answered,

361) 1 Timothy 3:16.
362) Colossians 1:15-17.
363) Sura *Maryam* 19:71, author's translation.

"Even me, except with a forgiveness from Allah."

In other words, he was just a regular sinful man like every-one else.[364] Muhammad could not heal, could not create, and could not raise the dead. Neither Muhammad, nor any other prophet, could do the miracles Christ Jesus did because Jesus Christ is the *Creator* who has His divine works, and all others are *creatures*, and they have their earthly works. There is no comparison.

The Holy Trinity in the Qur'an

The Qur'an did definitely confirm and speak in that verse[365] of the deity and divinity of Christ. However, the Qur'an also did the same thing in many other verses. The Qur'an even gave an excellent picture of the Holy Trinity:

"Christ Jesus, the son of Mary, an apostle of God, and His Word, which He bestowed on Mary, and a Spirit proceeding from Him."[366]

In this verse, God is speaking about His Word, namely, Jesus, and His Spirit. That adds up to God the Father, God the Son, and God the Holy Spirit, in One God. How could that be? Simple. When you multiply 1x1x1 it will equal 1. In that verse, the Qur'an cites the Bible in its own style and its own way of expression. Unfortunately, the Qur'an is not faithful in all its quotations from the Bible.

The center of the Qur'an is the person of Christ. The lost sheep in the Qur'an are the children of Israel, of whom Christ said:

364) In fact, according to the *Hadith* of Sahih Bukhari (Vol. 2, Book 23, #334; Vol. 5, Book 58, #266; and Vol. 9, Book 87, #131), Muhammad said, "By Allah, though I am the Apostle of Allah, yet I do not know what Allah will do to me" (meaning after he died).
365) Sura *Al-Imran* (the House of Imran) 3:49, mentioned above.
366) Sura *An-Nisa'* (the Women) 4:171.

"I am not sent but unto the lost sheep of the house of Israel."[367]

However, the *extra* things that were added to the Bible references in the Qur'an were really the special daily occurrences of Muhammad's life and lusts. Unfortunately, the one who quoted the Bible (Muhammad) in the Qur'an was not well acquainted with Bible stories and teachings. Those fractional Bible stories that were recorded in the Qur'an are referred to by Muslims as "the stories of the prophets."

For example, Muhammad took the fasting and the tithing from the Old Testament, but because of his lack of knowledge, he distorted them. When he discussed men's and women's rights, women were given half of what men have in all things. Why? No one knows.

The name of Jesus Christ appears in the Qur'an 25 times, mainly in the following Suras: *Al-Baqara* (2), *Al-Imran* (3), *Maryam* (19), *Al-Mu'minun* (23) and *Al-Hadid* (57).

Faith in the One God

The Qur'an verse that attracted my attention – and the attention of every Muslim who reads the Qur'an – is:

"The Creator of the heavens and the earth, how can he have a son, when He hath no consort (concubine), He created all things, and He is All-knowing."[368]

This verse carries the accusation that Christians have added a partner to God. Moreover, they assume that Christians teach that God had sexual relations with a woman, which resulted in the birth of a son. What a gross and disgusting misunderstanding, and what an atrocious assumption against Christians!

---

367) Matthew 15:24.
368) Sura *Al-An'am* (the Cattle) 6:101, author's translation.

The above-quoted verse is the sedative Muslims are taking to avoid the truth of the holy Trinity. Regrettably, I was one of those millions of Muslims who had that awful misconception. But when I discovered that the claims of the Qur'an against the Bible and Christianity were false, I knew that I was deceived, as hundreds of millions of Muslims are now. Now I know the truth. Christians do not believe that atrocity, and they have never taught it. On the contrary, Christianity denounces and condemns such teaching.

The Bible clearly teaches that there is one God. The Torah declares the oneness of God:

"Hear O Israel, the Lord our God is One Lord."[369]

The Lord was quoted by one of the greatest prophets:

"I am the Lord, and there is none else, there is no God beside me."[370]

The Gospel followed to confirm the teachings of the Torah and the Old Testament on the doctrine of the oneness of God. Paul the Apostle wrote to the Ephesians that Christians believe in "One Lord, one faith..."[371] And he wrote to his son in the faith, Timothy:

"For there is one God, and one Mediator between God and men...."[372]

The Lord Jesus Christ taught the same doctrine:

"Ye do err, not knowing the scriptures, nor the power of God." "... have you not read what was that which was spoken unto you by God, I am the God of Abraham...?" "Thou shalt love the Lord thy God

369) Deuteronomy 6:4.
370) Isaiah 45:5.
371) Ephesians 4:5.
372) 1 Timothy 2:5.

with all thy heart, with all thy soul, and with all thy mind."[373]

Then Jesus taught His disciples an important lesson:

"And call no one your father upon the earth, for one is your Father, which is in heaven."[374]

Then the Lord Jesus Christ Himself insisted on teaching that there is one God:

"There is none good but one, that is God."[375]

Christ went on to teach his hearers an important lesson that the Muslims ignored about Christianity:

"The first of all the commandments is, Hear, O Israel, the Lord our God is one Lord. And thou shalt love the Lord thy God with all thy heart... And the scribe said unto him, Well, Master, thou hast said the truth: for there is one God, and there is none other but He."[376]

Faith in the Holy Trinity

Some people contend that Christians believe in the Trinity of God; i.e., One God in three persons. They ask, How can you believe that there is one in three and three in one? Is that logical? The question is easy, really easy. This universe and everything in it is made to reflect the tri-unity of the Triune God. That is why, from the small atom to the huge suns, they are made in trinities. You cannot find one item in this universe that is not one in three and three in one.

The atom is made of neutron, proton and electron: three in one and one in three. Is that logical or not? How can

---

373) See Matthew 22:29-37.
374) Matthew 23:9.
375) Mark 10:18.
376) See Mark 12:29-32.

we accept the trinitarian nature of the objects all around us, yet we reject the Trinity of God? Christians believe that the Holy Trinity is a composite one God in three persons, God the Father, God the Son and God the Holy Ghost. The Three are One, as man is Body, Spirit and Soul. The three are one. For this reason, Christ could say: "I and my Father are one."[377] He insisted that because He is one with the Father, He is the only means to reach the Father:

"I am the way, the truth and the life: no man cometh unto the Father but by me."[378]

Christians cannot be accused of adding a partner to God. When I entered the fold, I could understand that Christianity teaches the Oneness of God more faithfully than any other religion. It is blasphemy, condemned by Christians, to say that God married a woman and begat a child from her.

However, Islam and Moslem sheikhs have ingrained in the Muslim public that Christians are promoting a partner to God. The Qur'an says:

"Say, He is Allah, the One and Only; Allah, the Eternal, Absolute; He begetteth not, nor is He begotten; and there is none like unto Him."[379]

Christianity believes in one God who was not born and did not have a wife. God is not flesh with man's needs. Men die. God does not die. People are stricken with diseases and sicknesses. God is above all that. Rather, He heals the sick, raises the dead, and creates. He is our Father in heaven. When people think superficially, they differ with Christianity about the nature of God. Why then do Muslim sheikhs wrongfully accuse Christians of blaspheming God's name?

377) John 10:30.
378) John 14:6.
379) Sura *Al-Ikhlas* (the Unity) 112:1-4.

Who Made up Partners for God?

Regrettably, what every bowl overflows is what it contains. Islam's teachings and Muslim indoctrination, as they developed during the formation of Islam as a religion, clearly prove that the only ones who have made infamous partners to God were Islam and the Muslims – definitely *not* the Christians!

The Qur'an acknowledged that Muhammad was only human as the rest of mankind. Despite that fact, Muhammad places himself *with* God and making himself *equal* to God.

For example, a person cannot be a Muslim unless he utters the Two Testimonies: "I testify that there is no god but Allah," and "I testify that Muhammad is the Messenger of Allah." This means that Islam is literally Allah + Muhammad. Only when one confesses faith in Allah *and* Muhammad can he/she become a Muslim. Believing in Allah alone is not sufficient. It has to be Allah *and* Muhammad. Thus Islam has made a human, Muhammad, as a partner to God. *That is an unforgivable blasphemy*, even in Islam. Here, Islam turns around and <u>commits the very sin it condemns</u>.

Muhammad: the Partner of God?

Muhammad did not just commit that blatant sin. He went further in his arrogance: to make himself a *partner* of God in words and deeds! For example, Muhammad claimed that the Qur'an is the word of God; therefore it becomes the duty of every Muslim to abide by it. But he made himself also *equal* to God, and forced *himself* upon the Muslims and made *his* words the duty and responsibility of every Muslim to obey – or else.

The partnership of Muhammad to God in deeds was evident and manifested in the duties and responsibilities that are placed on Muslims. Muhammad's god has imposed upon the Muslims some duties that are required to be performed by Muslims to continue to be faithful and to be rewarded. But Muhammad also imposed upon Muslims his own rituals, called in Arabic, *Al-Sunnah*. Whoever follows them will have his rewards.

For example, Muhammad's god imposes upon Muslims to kneel twice during the dawn prayers. Muhammad added, in *Al-Hadith*, two other kneelings. For the noon prayer, Muhammad's god imposed four kneelings. Muhammad, in his charity, added another four kneelings to the noon prayer. The same happened with the rest of the daily prayers. As for fasting, Muhammad's god imposed upon Muslims to fast the month of Ramadan, which is a full month per year. But Muhammad had imposed more days, in addition to the law of his god. Therefore, whoever fasted the month of Ramadan will have his reward but whoever fasts according to Muhammad's added *Sunnah* will have extra rewards.

Even in prayers and supplications, Muhammad receives the lion's share. Also in the Abrahamic prayers, Muhammad's name must be mentioned. In all that, Muhammad was placing himself next to Allah as his partner, making his commands coequal with his god's. He did all that at the same time he acknowledged that he was a human, and confessed that he was a sinner who needed forgiveness of his past and future sins. How could a human, under sin, impose his words upon mankind, as though they are coequal to God's? How could a sinful human elevate his name to stand right beside the name of God who created him, and who will judge him? I wonder what kind of a judgment a man such will face on the Judgment Day?

Ironically, Muslims, in their prayers, seem to seek to mediate for Muhammad. At the mere mention of Muhammad's name, every Muslim is supposed to pray for Muhammad, saying: "May Allah pray upon him and grant him peace." صلى الله عليه وسلّم All prophets are considered advocates for the people. But Muhammad, in his arrogance, is the only prophet who asked his own followers to pray for him, so that Allah would hear the supplications on his behalf out of the hundreds of millions of people, and have mercy on him. Muhammad and his followers have ignored the fact that "it is appointed unto men once to die," after which is the judgment.[380] And no amount of prayer or supplication can change the eternal destiny of a sinner after he dies.

So who are the ones who blasphemously give a partner to God, Christians or Muslims? I put this question before all people, especially those who have gone astray and followed a mirage.

---

380) See Hebrews 9:27

8

The Cross and The Crucified

Jesus Christ came to earth with one ultimate purpose: to die on the cross of Calvary to satisfy divine justice on behalf of mankind. The only way to satisfy God's justice is for guilty, sinful man to die for his own sin, or for a sinless person to take his place to redeem him. Thus, Christ, perfect and sinless, against whom the law had no demand, became the Lamb of God, the sacrifice for the atonement and the redemption of mankind. In this regard, the Lord Jesus Christ declared about His coming to this earth:

> "For even the son of man came not to be ministered unto, but to minister, and to give his life a ransom for many."[381]

Christ came to earth to redeem lost sinners. People get saved by faith, looking to Christ, who was crucified for their sins. The Lord gave us this example. When the children of Israel were in the wilderness after they left Egypt, they sinned against the Lord. God sent snakes to bite them and inject their venom into them. When Moses prayed for

---

381) Mark 10:45.

his people, God commanded him to put a brass serpent on the hill, and whoever was bitten, and looked up at it, he/she would not die. But they had to turn to look at it.

The same is true of Christ, who was crucified on the cross on the hill of Calvary. Whosoever looks up to Christ, believing that He is the Lamb of God who died as an atonement for his sin, will be ransomed. Thus Christ said:

> "And as Moses lifted up the serpent in the wilderness, even so must the son of man be lifted up: that whosoever believeth in him should not perish, but have eternal life."[382]

To emphasize that He came to earth with the sole purpose of dying as the Lamb of God, the sacrifice for your sins and the sins of the world, Christ said:

> "Verily, verily, I say unto you, Except a corn of wheat fall into the ground and die, it abideth alone: but if it die, it bringeth forth much fruit."[383]

The Old Testament, written hundreds of years before Jesus Christ came to earth, predicted the death of Christ on the cross. Those prophecies were given by the prophets and the writers of the Psalms, and were well-known by the Jews who read the Bible. When Christ came to earth, those prophecies were fulfilled.[384]

Exodus chapter 12 speaks of the Passover Lamb that was sacrificed to redeem the first-born of the Israelites. That Passover Lamb was a symbol of the Lamb of God, the Lord Jesus Christ, who was to be the sacrifice for the atonement of the sins of the world and the redemption of all men.

---

382) John 3:14-15.
383) John 12:24.
384) For more prophecies on Christ's death, see Isaiah 53, Psalms 18, 22.

Christ's death on the cross was an undeniable, historical event witnessed by Jews, Gentiles and the disciples of Christ. It was also reported by many contemporary historians who were not Christians. Even many Muslim Imams, such as Ibn Abbas, Muhammad bin Ishaq, Wahab and Rabi' bin Uns acknowledged Christ's death.

The Qur'an affirmed the death and resurrection of Christ, as though it were confirming this undeniable fact. It says, as though quoting Christ:

"So peace is on me the day I was born, the day that I die, and the day that I shall be raised up to life (again)!"[385]

The Qur'an continues, as though quoting God, who was assuring Christ that He would die and rise again:

"Behold, Allah said, O Jesus, I will take thee (in Arabic: متوفيك "I will cause thee to die") and raise thee to myself, and clear (purify) thee of those who disbelieve; and I will make those who followed thee superior to those who reject faith, to the Day of Resurrection."[386]

Also, the Qur'an supposedly quotes Christ, saying to God:

"When Thou didst take me up (in Arabic: "when thou didst cause me to die"), Thou wast the watcher over them."[387]

First, those who know Arabic and read the translation of the Qur'an in English, wonder: "Why did the translators change the words so drastically as they were translating? They perverted the word that means "cause to die" into "take up." Why?"

---

385) Sura *Maryam* 19:33.
386) Sura *Al-Imran* (the House of Imran) 3:55.
387) Sura *Al-Ma'idah* (the Table) 5:117.

Regardless, it seems very clear to the readers of those Arabic verses of the Qur'an that Christ was born, He died and rose from the dead. Then the Qur'an, as usual, contradicts itself when it makes the statement in *only one place*:

> "That they [the Jews] said (in boast), We killed Christ Jesus the son of Mary, the messenger of Allah. But they killed him not, nor crucified him, but so it was made to appear to them...."[388]

If this verse means what most Muslim scholars understand it to mean, then the god of Muhammad has registered two contradictory opinions, and "Gabriel" carried to Muhammad verses that contradict themselves.

The question is, Did Christ die or not? Was He crucified or wasn't He? The Qur'an says that Christ died, then it contradicts itself, saying He did not die; that He was crucified, and that He was not crucified. Muslim scholars can give no answers concerning these contradictions because they are dumbfounded!

As one reads the Qur'an, he/she finds that the death of Christ is an undeniable fact, as long as Sura *An-Nisa'* 4:157 is excluded, where Muhammad clearly contradicts himself. Why did he? In the beginning of his calling[389] Muhammad was weak, and needed the sympathy of Christians, such as Khadija bint Khuwaylid, his first wife, who was a Christian,[390] and her uncle, the Reverend Waraqa Ibn Nawfal, Muhammad's primary source of Bible knowledge. So early on, his writing tried to appease the Christian faith. *But as soon as Muhammad established himself in Medina, where he built his military and political power, he changed his stand – and*

---

388) Sura *An-Nisa'* (the Women) 4:157.
389) That is, in the years he lived in Mecca.
390) *Christian* – see Chapter 1, Footnote #7 for more information.

his friends – and contradicted everything he had previously said. (This is another example of Muhammad's "Annulling-and-Annulled" verses).

Even though the Qur'an has many verses about the death of Christ, regrettably Muslims mainly memorize the only one that contradicts the rest of the verses: "But they killed him not, nor crucified him." But if Christ was not crucified, why did Muhammad specify that kind of death (the crucifixion), when the Jews had never crucified anyone, but rather stoned the guilty ones? This is the most quoted verse in discussions between Christians and Muslims on the subject of Christ's death. Why not the other verses?

In Medina, Muhammad was free to say whatever he wanted; and the angel of Muhammad also had the freedom to bring down to him whatever self-contradictory verses he wanted. However, Muhammad had no right to force us to believe the changes he made in history. Further, Muhammad, his god and his angel had the right to contradict each other, but they cannot make us believe what they said because we have minds that can discern the truth (or lack thereof) in the Qur'an.

I place all these contradictions in the lap of Muslims so they may question their scholars. Or maybe those scholars can come up with *another* meaning for the word "death," as did so many translators of the Qur'an.

9

Was the Bible Altered?

In chapter two, we showed how ambiguities in the text of the Qur'an and the confusion in its compilation make it impossible for us to believe that the Qur'an was sent by God.

It is also impossible to believe, after studying Muhammad's life, that he was a prophet of God.

In this chapter, we will discuss accusations Muslims make against the Bible. Muslims are widely taught that the Bible has been changed, even though the Lord Jesus declared:

"Heaven and earth shall pass away, but my words shall not pass away."[391]

Isaiah described the Word of God:

"The grass withereth, the flower fadeth: but the word of our God shall stand for ever."[392]

The Psalms quoted God Himself:

"My covenant will I not break, nor alter the thing that is gone out of my lips."[393]

---

391) See Matthew 24:35; Mark 13:31; & Luke 21:33.
392) Isaiah 40:8. See also 1 Peter 1:24-25.
393) Psalm 89:34.

Matthew quotes Christ:

"For verily I say unto you, Till heaven and earth pass, one jot or one tittle shall in no wise pass from the law, till all be fulfilled."[394]

The book of Deuteronomy says:

"Ye shall not add unto the word which I command, neither shall ye diminish ought from it, that ye may keep the commandments of the Lord your God, which I commanded you."[395]

Jeremiah declared:

"Then said the Lord unto me, Thou hast well seen: for I will hasten my word to perform it."[396]

The wisest man who ever lived, King Solomon, said:

"Every word of God is pure: he is a shield unto them that put their trust in him. Add thou not unto his words, lest he reprove thee, and thou be found a liar."[397]

The Lord Himself gave an awesome warning in the last paragraph of the last book of the Bible:

"For I testify unto every man that heareth the words of the prophecy of this book, if any man shall add unto these things, God shall add unto him the plagues that are written in this book: And if any man shall take away from the words of the book of this prophecy, God shall take away his part out of the book of life, and out of the holy city, and from the things which are written in this book."[398]

---

394) Matthew 5:18.
395) Deuteronomy 4:2.
396) Jeremiah 1:12.
397) Proverbs 30:5-6.
398) Revelation 22:18-19.

These are a few from a battery of verses that assure us God's words do not pass away. Moreover, they assure us that God does not annul or change His words, as often happened in the Qur'anic verses. In fact, the Qur'an confirms that Allah <u>does</u> change his mind and annul his words. At the same time Muhammad's god changes his words and annuls his verses, he contradicts himself:

> "We have, without doubt, sent down the Message [the remembrance or the Qur'an] and We will assuredly guard it (from corruption)."[399] Jonah X: 64).

This verse and many others in the Qur'an prove, without a doubt, that the Bible is the word of God.

The preserved words of God go all the way back to the Syrian Peshitta and the Old Latin, the oldest translations ever, written about 150 AD in Antioch of Syria.[400] From the preserved manuscripts, thousands of copies and translations were made and can be compared, assuring that we have an accurate text. By them the King James Bible was translated to English.[401]

Even the Arabs who studied the Bible in the olden days, such as Reverend Nawfal and his niece, Khadija bint Khuwaylid, knew well that the Bible was (and is) infallible. The Qur'an, coupled with Muhammad's limited Bible knowledge, attempted to quote the Bible. If there were any alterations in the Bible, Muhammad would not have attempted to quote from it and what's more, he would not have said

---

399) Sura *Al-Hijr* (the Rock) 15:9. See also *Yunus* (Jonah) 10:64.

400) Where the disciples were first called Christians. See Acts 11:26.

401) Throughout history, God has preserved His words by the persecuted believers (not the Roman Catholic system). The King James Bible is the English testimony to this preservation. For more on the Alexandrian vs. the preserved Bibles, see *Did the Catholic Church Give Us the Bible?* and *Answers to Your Bible Version Questions*, from Chick Publications.

that Christians would stand on nothing unless they upheld the Bible.[402]

The Qur'an continued to confirm the fact that the Bible is the word of God and is true because it is from God. No one could change anything in the original Bible text because they could not then and they cannot now. The *true* God preserved *His* words. We cannot say the same for Allah.

Other manuscripts that prove the infallibility of God's word are the following:

1. The Oxyrhynchus and other papyri,[403] found in the sands of Egypt. Some manuscripts, such as one with fragments of the Gospel of John, have been dated at 125 AD or earlier.[404]

2. The manuscripts of Qumran, which are real Biblical treasures that were found by a young Jordanian shepherd in 1947. Those manuscripts were written from 250 BC to ca. 68 AD, in the old Hebrew language. The first book of the Bible to be discovered among those manuscripts was the book of Isaiah. After the news of the discovery of Isaiah, a British team was sent to Qumran to excavate. There, they found the greatest surprise ever – all or part of every book of the Old Testament except Nehemiah. The scholars confirmed that the texts of those books are in total agreement with the text of the Bible that is in our hands today, even

---

402) See Sura *Al-Ma'idah* (the Table) 5:68.

403) Papyrus is a plant from which early "paper" was made.

404) The manuscript of portions of John 18 is called "John Rylands Papyrus (52)" It was the earliest known – that is, until the Magdalene Papyrus (P64) of portions of Matthew 26 was dated at before 66 AD (and backing the KJV text)! For dating and text, see *Eyewitness to Jesus* by Carsten Thiede & Matthew D'Ancona (1996), pp. 115 and 125; and *The Text of the Earliest New Testament Greek Manuscripts* by Comfort & Barrett (1999), pp.365-368.

though they were written more than two hundred years before Christ. Before them, the oldest Hebrew Bible we possessed was dated 1,000 AD.[405]

3. Historical excavations done by many scholars in the
field, along with many international teams, looking for material evidence in the lands of Palestine and Mesopotamia,
have further proven the soundness of the Holy Bible.

4. To Muslims who accuse Christians and Jews of altering
and changing the Bible, I say: Islam and its Qur'an have testified of the soundness of the Holy Scriptures. The Qur'an
bears a clear witness of the infallibility of the Bible:

> "They have the Law wherein is the judgment of
> God... It was therein we revealed (sent down) the
> Law (the Torah); therein there was (is) guidance and
> light; by its standard have been judged the Jews, by
> the prophets (by its standards the prophets issued
> their judgment)... For to them was entrusted the
> protection of God's book."[406]

The Qur'an continues in the same Sura:

> "And in their footsteps we sent Jesus the son of
> Mary, confirming the Law that had come before
> him. We sent him the Gospel: therein was [is] guid-
> ance and light, and confirmation of the Law that
> had come before him: a guidance and admonition to
> those who fear God."[407]

Also, the Qur'an assures that the Gospel teachings are to
be followed. The following Qur'anic verse urges Christians
to abide by its teachings:

---

405) For more information, see *The Dead Sea Scrolls Bible*, translation and
commentary by Abegg, Flint & Ulrich (1999)
406) Sura *Al-Ma'idah* (the Table) 5:43-44, author's translation.
407) Sura *Al-Ma'idah* 5:46.

"Say, O People of the Book! You have no ground to stand upon unless ye stand fast by [uphold] the Law [the Torah] and the Gospel..."[408]

Here's another Qur'an verse on the Bible:

"O ye who believe! Believe in Allah and his apostle (Muhammad), and the scripture which he hath sent to his apostle and the scripture which he sent to those before (him). Any who denieth God, his angels, his Books, his apostles [messengers], and the Day of Judgment, hath gone far, far astray."[409]

The Qur'an says this about the people of the Torah:

"These were the men to whom we gave the Book, and authority, and prophethood: if these (their descendants) reject them, Behold! We shall entrust their charge to a new people who reject them not. Those who were (the prophets) who received God's guidance: copy the guidance they received. Say, 'No reward for this do I ask of you: This is no less than a message for the nations.'"[410]

How could Muslims accuse Christians of altering their Book at the very time the god of the Qur'an urged Muhammad to turn to the Bible when he needed help understanding something spiritual? Would Muhammad be pointed towards the Bible if it was altered? The Qur'an says:

"And before thee also the messengers [apostles] We sent were but men, to whom We granted inspiration: if ye realize not, ask of those who possess the Message [Christians and Jews]."[411]

---

408) Sura *Al-Ma'idah* 5:68.
409) Sura *An-Nisa'* (the Women) 4:136.
410) Sura *Al-An'am* (the Cattle) 6:89-90.
411) Sura *An-Nahl* (the Bee) 16:43.

More than all that, the Qur'an confirmed to Muhammad that when he had any doubts, fears or confusion concerning his knowledge, he should resort to the Bible:

> "If thou wert in doubt as to what We have revealed unto thee, then ask those who have been reading the Book from before thee [the Jews and the Christians]."[412]

Furthermore, the Qur'an testifies of the rightness and truth of the Bible, affirming that it has been protected by God, proving that it is a book from God. Therefore, all its books are completely infallible and in total harmony.

The Qur'an says:

> "We have without doubt, sent down the Message (the remembrance); and we will assuredly guard it."[413]

> "…There is none that can alter the words of God…"[414]

> "The word of thy Lord doth find its fulfillment in truth and in justice: None can change His words…."[415]

> "Say ye, We believe in God, and the revelation given to us, and to Abraham, Ishmael, Isaac, Jacob, and the tribes, and that given to Moses and Jesus, and that given to (all) prophets from their Lord: We make no difference between one and another of them: And we bow to God."[416]

This is a clear testimony of the Qur'an in favor of the Bible, yet Muslims claim it has been altered and changed. Was it not the true God who inspired the Bible? God is

---

412) Sura *Yunus* (Jonah) 10:94.
413) Sura *Al-Hijr* (the Rock) 15:9.
414) Sura *Al-An'am* (the Cattle) 6:34, author's translation.
415) Sura *Al-An'am* 6:115.
416) Sura *Al-Baqara* (the Cow) 2:136, author's translation.

able to protect and guard the Book He inspired! The question we should ask is, "Why wasn't Allah able to protect the Qur'an?"

10

How The Qur'an Distorts The Bible

In this chapter you will see how some of the most famous Bible stories are distorted in the Qur'an.

The First Story: Abram who Became Abraham

The Story of Abraham was recorded in the Torah. Beginning with Genesis 11, it discusses human ancestry back to Shem, the son of Noah. Therefore, Abraham is a descendant of Shem. In chapter twelve, God commanded Abraham to leave Haran.

The Bible says:

> "So Abram (whose name was later changed by God to Abraham) departed, as the Lord had spoken unto him, and Lot went with him: and Abram was seventy and five years when he departed out of Haran."[417]

Abram took with him Sarai, his wife. Both men, Abram and Lot, were very wealthy men, each possessing a very great herd of cattle and sheep. After their arrival in the land of Canaan, a famine struck the land.

"And there was a famine in the land, and Abram

---

417) Genesis 12:4.

went down to Egypt to sojourn there: for the famine was grievous in the land."[418]

In Egypt, because he feared for his life, Abram told his wife to say that she was his sister, thinking that if they knew that she was his wife, they would kill him, seeing she was very beautiful.

Thus, Abram asked Sarai:

"Say, I pray thee, thou art my sister; that it may be well with me for thy sake; and my soul shall live because of thee."[419]

What he expected happened. Pharaoh sent his men to accompany Sarai to his palace, and he gave Abram much wealth because of Sarai. Pharaoh must have attempted to allure Sarai into his chamber:

"And the Lord plagued Pharaoh and his house with great plagues because of Sarai Abram's wife. And Pharaoh called Abram, and said, What is this that thou hast done unto me? Why didst thou not tell me that she was thy wife? Why saidst thou, She is my sister? So I might have taken her to me to wife: now therefore behold thy wife, take her, and go thy way. And Pharaoh commanded his men concerning him, and they sent him away, and his wife, and all that he had."[420]

Abram returned to Palestine, where God said to him:

"Arise, walk through the land in the length of if and in the breadth of it; for I will give it unto thee. Then Abram removed his tent, and came and dwelt in the

---

418) Genesis 12:10.
419) Genesis 12:13.
420) Genesis 12:17-20.

plain of Mamre, which is in Hebron, and built there
an altar unto the Lord."[421]

Abram settled in Hebron, which is now known as *Al-
Khalil* (meaning the friend of God, named after Abraham),
where his altar and his grave still exist.

Abraham had a strong relationship with the Lord, and
they both often carried on friendly conversations. Once,
Abram said to God:

> "Lord, God, what wilt thou give me, seeing I go
> childless, and the steward of my house is Eliezer of
> Damascus… Behold to me thou hast given no seed,
> and, lo, one born in my house (a servant) is mine
> heir."[422]

This was because his wife, Sarah, was barren and could not
give birth to children. Consequently, Sarah asked Abraham
to marry a bondmaid named Hagar, who was given to her by
Pharaoh when she was in Egypt, so she could give him the
awaited son, who would be named Ishmael.

The Bible says:

> "And Sarai Abram's wife took Hagar her maid the
> Egyptian … and gave her to her husband Abram,
> to be his wife. And he went in unto Hagar, and she
> conceived: and when she saw that she had conceived,
> her mistress was despised in her eyes. And Sarai said
> unto Abram, My wrong be upon thee: I have given
> my maid into thy bosom; and when she saw that
> she had conceived, I was despised in her eyes…. But
> Abram said unto Sarai, Behold, thy maid is in thy
> hand; do to her as it pleaseth thee."[423]

---

421) Genesis 13:17-18.
422) Genesis 15:2-4.
423) Genesis 16:3-6.

As a result, Sarai dealt so harshly with Hagar that she ran away.

> "And the angel of the Lord found her by the fountain of water in the wilderness, by the fountain in the way to Shur. And he said, Hagar, Sarai's maid, whence camest thou? And whither wilt thou go? And she said, I flee from the face of my mistress Sarai."[424]

However, the angel of the Lord commanded her to go back, where she gave birth to her child, and called his name Ishmael. When Ishmael was born, Abram was 86 years old.

About thirteen years later, when Abram was 99 years old, the angel of the Lord appeared to him to promise him the birth of his son from Sarai who was at that time 90 years old. Also, in that chapter, Genesis 17, the Lord:

• Promised Abram's son would be born in one year.

• Changed Abram's name into Abraham.

• Changed his wife's name from Sarai into Sarah.

The story continues:

> "And Sarah saw the son of Hagar the Egyptian, which she had born unto Abraham, mocking. Wherefore, she said unto Abraham, Cast out this bondwoman and her son: for the son of this bondwoman shall not be heir with my son, even with Isaac."[425]

When Abraham showed his frustration at the request of Sarah concerning Hagar, God appeared to him and commanded him to listen to Sarah.

> "And Abraham rose up early in the morning, and took bread, and a bottle of water, and gave it unto

---

424) Genesis 16:7-8.
425) Genesis 21:9-10.

Hagar, putting it on her shoulder, and the child, and sent her away: and she departed, and wandered in the wilderness of Beersheba. And the water was spent in the bottle, and she cast the child under one of the shrubs. And she went, and sat her down over against him a good way off, as it were a bowshot: for she said, Let me not see the death of the child. And she sat over against him, and lift her voice and wept. And God heard the voice of the lad; and the angel of God called to Hagar out of heaven, and said unto her, What aileth thee, Hagar? Fear not, for God hath heard the voice of the lad where he is. Arise, lift up the lad, and hold him in thine hand; for I will make him a great nation. And God opened her eyes, and she saw a well of water; and she went, and filled the bottle with water, and gave the lad drink. And God was with the lad; and he grew, and dwelt in the wilderness, and became an archer. And he dwelt in the wilderness of Paran: and his mother took him a wife out of the land of Egypt (a woman from Hagar's homeland)."[426]

When Isaac was about fourteen years old, the Lord demanded Abraham to take Isaac to Mount Moriah where he should offer his beloved son as a sacrifice to God. Abraham obeyed, and when Abraham and Isaac...

"...came to the place which God had told him of; and Abraham built an altar there, and laid the wood in order, and bound Isaac his son, and laid him on the altar upon the wood. And Abraham stretched forth his hand, and took the knife to slay his son. And the angel of the Lord called unto him out of

426) Genesis 21:14-21.

heaven, and said, Abraham, Abraham: and he said, Here am I. And he said, Lay not thy hand upon the lad, neither do thou any thing unto him: for now I know that thou fearest God, seeing thou hast not withheld thy son, thine only son from me. And Abraham lifted up his eyes, and looked, and behold behind him a ram caught in a thicket by his horns: and Abraham went and took the ram, and offered him up for a burnt offering in the stead of his son. And Abraham called the name of that place Jehovah-jireh, as it is said to this day, In the mount of the Lord it shall be seen."[427]

Sarah lived until she was 127 years old, and she "died in Kir-jath-arba; the same is Hebron in the land of Canaan"[428] (close to the city of *Al-Khalil*, where the Jews built a settlement called Kir-jath-arba, in honor of Sarah's burial place.)

After the death of Sarah, Abraham took a wife whose name was Keturah:

"And she bare him Zimran, and Jokshan, and Medan, and Midian, and Ishbak, and Shuah."[429]

When Abraham died, he was 175 years old.

"And his sons Isaac and Ishmael buried him in the cave of Machpelah, in the field of Ephron the son of Zohar the Hittite, which is before Mamre."[430]

Two points are important:

1. Abraham lived all of his life in Palestine after leaving Haran, except for a brief visit to Egypt. He *never* visited the Arabian Peninsula.

---

427) Genesis 22:9-14.
428) Genesis 23:2.
429) Genesis 25:2.
430) Genesis 25:9.

2. Ishmael never lived in the Arabian Peninsula either, but close to his father, which allowed him to be at his father's funeral.

Those who would like to know more about the life Abraham should read the book of Genesis from chapters 11 through 25. And remember, the Torah was written more than 2000 years before Muhammad and the Qur'an. So let's find out: Did the Qur'an recite the story of Abraham as it was recorded in the Bible, or did it distort the facts?

Abraham's Story in the Qur'an

Here is what the Qur'an and its interpreters said about Abraham, Sarah, and the two sons, Ishmael and Isaac.

Abd Al-Hamid Al-Sahhar wrote that Abraham lived in Babylon (not Ur) and that his father, whose name was Aazar (not Terah), was a trader, selling idols in the markets and the worship places. But Abraham refused to sell idols.[431] The Qur'an says on that subject:

> "And rehearse [recite] to them (something of) Abraham's story. Behold, he said to his father and his people, 'What worship ye?' They said, 'We worship idols, and we remain constantly in attendance on them.'"[432]

Then Abraham, according to Islamic stories, resorted to the mountains seeking his God. After much toil in searching, he found the answer, which resulted in his coming back to town and smashing the idols. His people complained to King Nimrod,[433] who decided at a great feast to throw Abra-

---

431) *On the Margin of the Life of Muhammad* by Abd Al-Hamid Al-Sahhar, Vol. 1.

432) Sura *Ash-Shu'ara'* (the Poets) 26:69-71.

433) Nimrod, dead about 250 years, is totally out of place here.

ham in a furnace of fire.[434] The furnace was prepared, the fire was lit, and Abraham was thrown into the fire. However, the fire suddenly turned into coldness and peace for him, and he was not hurt because his God delivered him from the fire.

As a result to that experience, King Nimrod was struck with fear enough to release Abraham. But Abraham continued in his flight, accompanied with his cousin, Sarah, whom he took for a wife, and his nephew, Lot.

The story continues that before they entered Palestine, when he was on the border, south of the Jordan River, Pharaoh's soldiers took Sarah as captive. When Abraham knew that she was taken captive, he went to Pharaoh, who, as soon as he knew that he was a prophet of God, gave him cattle, horses, silver and gold. Pharaoh also freed Sarah, who declined Pharaoh's proposal, and he gave her one of his maids as her bondmaid, called Hagar.

Al-Hamid Al-Sahhar continued: Hagar the Egyptian was an educated woman, whose husband was the king of Southern Egypt, in an emirate called Manif. Pharaoh declared war against him and killed him, taking his wife, Princess Hagar, as a captive. Then Sarah and Hagar got acquainted while they both were in Pharaoh's prison. But when Abraham came to Egypt, Pharaoh released Sarah and presented Hagar to her as a gift. Abraham's whole party departed to Palestine where they settled in Hebron, in the town that was called later *Al-Khalil*.

Soon Sarah was in her seventies without giving birth to a child and continued to be barren. So she asked Abraham to marry her bondmaid, Hagar, that she might give him a child. What Sarah expected, happened; and Ishmael was born.

---

434) Confused with the 3 Hebrews (Daniel 3) 1500 years later!

Al-Sahhar proceeded in his book to claim that it was God who told Abraham to send Hagar with her child to another place. So Abraham walked from Hebron in Palestine with Hagar and Ishmael, the suckling, to Mecca. And the Qur'an described Mecca as a wilderness in those days:

> "O our Lord! I have made some of my offspring to dwell in a valley without cultivation, by thy sacred house; in order, O our Lord, that they may establish regular prayer: so till the hearts of some among men with love towards them, and feed them with fruits: so that they may give thanks."[435]

According to the Islamic story, Hagar asked Abraham the cause of the harsh treatment she received from him. He answered that what was happening was the will of God. She answered him: If that was the will of God, then let all power belong to Him.

Abraham returned to Hebron, where God gave him the good news that his wife, Sarah, was with child, whose name would be Isaac. At that time, Sarah was seventy years old. Abraham visited Mecca, where God commanded him to sacrifice Ishmael. When he attempted to do it, God redeemed Ishmael with a lamb.

Later, Ishmael married a Yemeni woman of the tribe of Gerham and settled in the Arabian Peninsula for the rest of his life. But Isaac settled in Palestine the rest of his days, where he begat Jacob, who begat Joseph and Benjamin. Also, the Qur'an mentions that Ishmael and Abraham were the ones who erected the pillars of the Ka'aba. For this reason, visitors and pilgrims to Mecca find there a shrine for Abraham.

---

435) Sura *Ibrahim* (Abraham) 14:37.

Al-Sahhar said in his book that Abraham got married at the age of 175, but he did not say if he begat any children. Abraham and Sarah died in Hebron, and were buried there. That is how the story of Abraham is recorded in the Qur'an. Here are some of those verses (the distortions are obvious):

In the following verse, God appointed Abraham as the Imam of the Ka'aba:

> "And remember that Abraham was tried by his Lord with certain commands, which he fulfilled: He said: 'I will make thee an Imam to the nations.' He pleaded: 'And also (Imams) from my offspring!' He answered: 'But my promise is not within the reach of evil doers."[436]

There is also a command from Allah in the Qur'an to Abraham and Ishmael to clear the Ka'aba:

> "Remember We made the house a place of assembly for men and a place of safety; and take ye the station of Abraham as a place of prayer; and We covenanted with Abraham and Ishmael, that they should sanctify my house for those who compass it round, or use it as a retreat, or bow, or prostrate themselves (therein in prayer)."[437]

The Qur'an records a command from Abraham to his sons to be Muslims (even though they lived more that two thousand years before Islam started):

> "And this is the legacy that Abraham left to his sons, and so did Jacob; 'Oh my sons! Allah hath chosen the Faith for you; then die not except in the Faith of Islam."[438]

---

436) Sura *Al-Baqara* (the Cow) 2:124.
437) Sura *Al-Baqara* 2:125.
438) Sura *Al-Baqara* 2:132.

How could such a statement be credible, when those people and their descendents were Jewish, and they lived thousands of years before Islam?

In the story of Zamzam, the Qur'an says Allah commanded As-Safa and Marwah[439] be made parts of the rituals of the pilgrimage. The story said that when Abraham left the infant, Ishmael, and his mother, Hagar, in the middle of the desert, Ishmael got thirsty and almost died. Hagar walked toward the south and toward the north seven times, then returned to her son, and found that water sprang from under his feet. Muslims call this the water of Zamzam.

Muhammad made the seven walks of Hagar looking for water as part of the Islamic pilgrimage rituals, saying in the Qur'an:

> "Behold! Safa and Marwah are among the Symbols [rituals] of Allah. So if those who visit the House [Ka'aba in Mecca] in the Season or at other times, should compass them round, it is no sin in them. And if any one obeyeth his own impulse to good—be sure that Allah is He Who recognizeth and knoweth."[440]

The Qur'an also insists that Abraham was a Muslim:

> "Abraham was not a Jew nor yet a Christian; but he was true in faith; and bowed his will to Allah's (which is Islam) and he joined not gods with Allah."[441]

Furthermore, the Qur'an assures us that Abraham was the first one to build the Ka'aba:

---

439) That is, running back and forth between these two hills of Mecca. For more information, see the end of Chapter 5.

440) Sura *Al-Baqara* 2:158.

441) Sura *Al-Imran* (the Family of Imran) 3:67.

"The first House (of worship) appointed for men was that at Bakka (Mecca): Full of blessing and guidance for all kinds of beings."[442]

The story of Abraham is scattered throughout the Qur'an in more than eighty verses that Al-Sahhar gathered into the story told above.

Now that you have seen the story from both sources, the many differences and distortions may be clearly displayed:

1. The Torah says that Abraham's wife was Sarai at the beginning of her life and that Abram's name was changed to Abraham. Abraham's father's name was Terah, and his brother's name was Nahor. The Bible makes it clear that Abraham and his father did not live in the days of Nimrod, nor does it say that Abraham was thrown in a furnace of fire that turned into coolness and safety.

On the contrary, the Qur'an gave Abraham's father a totally new and different name, Aazar.

2. The Torah explains that Hagar was a regular bondmaid – not a former princess, but Muslim scholars pictured Hagar as a princess of a territory south of Egypt who became a bondmaid after being taken captive by Pharaoh.

3. The Bible says that Abraham sent Hagar, his wife's bondmaid, and her son Ishmael, to a wilderness south of Palestine, close to Egypt, not far from Beersheba, where she later got a wife for her son. The Qur'an contradicted, saying she went to the Arabian Peninsula, specifically, to Mecca.

4. According to the Bible, Abraham moved around southern Palestine but never made it to Mecca. And he was definitely never involved in building the temple, where the Ka'aba is found, because it was a temple of idols. However,

---

442) Sura *Al-Imran* 3:96.

Muslims and their scholars claim the Qur'anic version, which says Abraham traveled with his son, Ishmael, all the way to Mecca to build the Ka'aba and its temple – *where 360 pagan idols stood!* Is that believable?

5. Furthermore, the Qur'an says that Abraham was not a Jew nor a Christian, but a fundamental Muslim. Was the "Islam" mentioned in the Qur'an a figure of speech or was it literal – that he was a Muslim, thousands of years before the coming of Islam?

6. The Qur'an insists that Abraham offered Ishmael, not Isaac, as a sacrifice and that the location was a mountain near Mecca. But the Bible, which is the origin of the story, insists that Isaac was put on the altar, built on Mount Moriah, a little north of Hebron, not far south in Arabia.

As Muslims, we have been taught by the Qur'an that the Bible is God's infallible word. Therefore, we should believe what it says. If we say the Bible was altered, the question is: Why? and for whose benefit? All the proofs state the contrary, that the Bible was never changed. Moreover, it is enough for us to take the testimony of the Qur'an that insists the Bible is infallible, stating that God sent down the Remembrance (the Bible) and that He is guarding it.

As a result, it becomes logical and imperative that we accept the Biblical account as the *original* source of the records. It was factually impossible for Ishmael and his mother to walk about 1,000 miles to Mecca. But it was easier for them to travel a few miles to southern Palestine, where they settled, not far away from Beersheba. It was close enough that Ishmael was there to attend his father's funeral. It would have been impossible to be at the funeral if he was a thousand miles away. How could he *hear* about the funeral if he was that far, let alone *attend?*

If we accept that the Biblical account is true, then most of the story in the Qur'an is grossly exaggerated or badly distorted. If we believe that the Bible is true *and* the Qur'an account is true, then we have two "Gods," one God of the Bible and the other who sent down the distorted stories of the Qur'an. But that is impossible, for the Bible and the Qur'an agree on this one point, that there is one God, not two. It should be obvious which book is true.

Joseph, the Son of Jacob

The Bible says Joseph began in a very rich home, where he was treated as the preferred son. His father Jacob, the prophet, loved him and showed him special treatment, like bringing him a coat of many colors. This special treatment provoked his brothers' jealousy. But when Joseph dreamed those strange dreams, whereby he was projected as the prince before whom his father, mother, and brethren would bow down, his brothers both envied and despised him.

One day, his father asked him to go see how his brothers were doing. When he came to their quarters, they caught him, put him in a nearby well and decided to get rid of him. Their brother, Judah, convinced them not to kill him, but sell him to an Ishmaelite caravan which was on its way to Egypt. In Egypt, he was sold to Potiphar, the captain of the guard, where he was well treated and became the general manager of the house of Potiphar.[443]

Potiphar's wife had her eyes on him, and asked him to lie with her.

> "But he refused, and said unto his master's wife, Behold, my master wotteth [knows] not what is with me in the house, and he hath committed all that he

443) See Genesis 37 & 39:1-6.

hath to my hand; There is none greater in this house than I; neither hath he kept back any thing from me but thee, because thou art his wife: how then can I do this great wickedness and sin against God?"[444]

One time, when he ran away from her, she grabbed his coat and he fled, leaving it in her hand. When her husband came home, she accused Joseph of attempting to rape her. Consequently, Joseph was arrested and thrown in prison.[445]

In prison he met the Pharaoh's chief baker and chief butler. By that time, and by God's grace, Joseph had become the manager of the prison. Those two chiefs dreamed dreams and asked Joseph for the interpretation. He told the butler that he would be restored to his office, but he told the baker he would be executed. And so it happened.[446]

Pharaoh later had an intense series of dreams. When no one could interpret his dream, the chief butler remembered Joseph's ability to interpret dreams. He mentioned him to his sovereign and Joseph was brought to the king. Joseph told the king the interpretation of his dreams: seven years of abundance followed by seven years of famine.

As a result, Joseph was made a top ruler in Egypt. He did such a great job of managing the situation that all of Egypt became the personal property of Pharaoh. Because of that famine, his brothers came to Egypt to buy the needed grains. When they entered into their brother's presence, they bowed down before him, the prince of Egypt, just like in Joseph's dreams![447] If you would like to read the full story, please go to the book of Genesis, chapters 37-50.

---

444) Genesis 39:8-9.
445) Genesis 39:10-20.
446) See Genesis 39:21-40:23.
447) These events are found in Genesis 40-50.

Joseph's Story in the Qur'an

The Qur'an did a great injustice, both to Joseph and his righteousness, and to the Bible, by grossly distorting this story. When the Qur'an came to the part of the temptation, as the woman attempted to seduce him, the Qur'an says:

> "And (with passion) did she desire him, and (with passion) did he desire her, [the Arabic word, همّت به وهمّ بها has a deeper meaning than just desiring with passion], but that he saw the evidence of his Lord...."[448]

Because Joseph saw the evidence of his Lord, he interrupted whatever he was doing with her, and attempted to run away. What evidence? No one really knows. But the Qur'an's distortion here is that he was responding to her sexual advances until he saw the evidence of his God. The Bible tells the true story: When she tried to seduce him, he did not even have to think about it. It says:

> "But he refused, and said unto his master's wife... how then can I do this great wickedness, and sin against God?"[449]

Solomon the King ... or the Prophet?

Solomon's life and accomplishments are recorded mainly in 2 Samuel 1-11. They are repeated in 1 Chronicles 1-9. Also, 1 Samuel 12 tells us the story of his birth.

It is important to note that Solomon was the son of David, the king of Israel. He was raised in the Jewish faith and followed in the footsteps of his father. He did great things for the Lord, and inherited the throne after David. He superseded his father in the faith, accomplishing what his fa-

---

448) Sura *Yusuf* (Joseph) 12:24, author's translation.
449) Genesis 39:9-10.

ther only wished he could. When God asked Solomon what he wanted most from Him, Solomon asked the Lord to give him wisdom. His request pleased the Lord. The Bible says:

> "And God said to him, Because thou hast asked this thing, and hast not asked for thyself long life; neither hast asked riches for thyself, nor hast asked for the life of thine enemies; but hast asked for thyself understanding to discern judgment; Behold, I have done according to thy words: lo, I have given thee a wise and understanding heart; so that there was none like thee before thee, neither after thee shall any arise like unto thee."[450]

God made Solomon the wisest man who ever lived. As a king, he ruled with justice, and his wisdom became well known around the world and in every generation.

God commanded Israel to build Him a temple at Jerusalem. King David collected most of the materials for the temple, but it was young Solomon who accomplished the task for the Lord in seven years.[451]

Solomon also ordered the building of a fleet that sailed the Mediterranean and the Red Sea to bring to Jerusalem the riches of the nations.[452] The queen of Sheba heard much about Solomon, his wisdom and his riches:

> "And she came to Jerusalem with a very great train, with camels that bare spices, and very much gold, and precious stones: and when she was come to Solomon, she communed with him of all that was in her heart. And Solomon told her all her questions. There was not any thing hid from the king, which he

---

450) 1 Kings 3:11-12.
451) See 1 Kings 6:38.
452) See 1 Kings 9:26-28.

told her not. And when the queen of Sheba had seen all Solomon's wisdom, and the house that he had built, and the meat of his table, and the sittings of his servants, and the attendance of his ministers, and their apparel, and his cupbearers, and his ascent by which he went up unto the house of the Lord; there was so more spirit in her. And she said to the king, It was a true report that I heard in mine own country of thy acts and of thy wisdom... Blessed be the Lord thy God which delighted in thee to set thee on the throne of Israel...."[453]

Regrettably, Solomon sinned against the Lord in his old age. He built temples for the worship of Ashtoreth, the goddess of the Zidonians, and Milcom, the god of the Ammonites, and for the gods of Egypt:

"And Solomon did evil in the sight of the Lord, and went not fully after the Lord, as did David his father"[454]

Consequently, the Lord judged Solomon:

"Forasmuch as this is done of thee, and thou hast not kept my covenant and my statutes, which I have commanded thee, I will surely rend the kingdom from thee, and will give it to thy servant."[455]

The Lord acted on His judgment by putting problems before Solomon. In the latter days of Solomon's life, the Lord stirred up Solomon's adversaries against him, such as Hadad the Edomite, Rezon the son of Eliadah, and Jeroboam his servant.[456] The Bible concludes:

453) See 1 Kings 10:1-9.
454) 1 Kings 11:6.
455) 1 Kings 11:11.
456) See 1 Kings 11:14-40.

"And the time that Solomon reigned in Jerusalem over all Israel was forty years. And Solomon slept with his fathers, and was buried in the city of David his father: and Rehoboam his son reigned in his stead."[457]

Solomon's Story in the Qur'an

Does the Qur'an story agree with the long-standing Biblical record? Let's examine the Qur'anic account:

1. In the Bible, Solomon was the wise king. In the Qur'an, Solomon is referred to as a prophet.

2. The Qur'an records that Solomon's powers gave him authority to manipulate and use the Jinns (Genies) and the birds.[458] He also could control the winds. Further, Solomon could talk to animals and insects. The Qur'an says:

"At length, when they came to a (lowly) valley of ants, one the ants said: 'O ye ants, get into your habitation, lest Solomon and his hosts, crush you (under foot) without knowing it.'"[459]

In this Sura, Solomon *talked* to the ants. He could *hear* the ants talking to each other, and he could *understand* their language, whatever that language was!

3. The Qur'an claims that Solomon also reigned over the birds of the world. No bird could do anything without the command of Solomon. The Qur'an continues:

"And he (meaning Solomon) took a muster of the birds; and he said: 'Why is it I see not the hoopoe? Or is he among the absentees'?"[460]

457) 1 Kings 11:42-43.
458) See Sura *An-Naml* (the Ant) 27:17.
459) Sura *An-Naml* 27:18.
460) Sura *An-Naml* 27:20.

In that Sura, Solomon threatened the hoopoe and would not forgive it until he gave him a good excuse. But what excuse was the hoopoe supposed to bring Solomon that would please him? According to the Qur'an:

"But the hoopoe tarried not far: he (came up and) said, I have compassed (territory) which thou hast not compassed, and I have come to thee from Saba with tidings true."[461]

The hoopoe went on to describe to Solomon that the queen of Sheba and her throne and subjects worship the sun instead of Allah. The Qur'an continued, saying that Solomon sent a letter with the hoopoe inviting the queen of Sheba and to her subjects to accept Islam. In a few seconds, the hoopoe took that letter and flew from Jerusalem to Sheba in Ethiopia, where it gave the letter to the queen. She called all her counselors and said to them:

"Go thou, with this letter of mine, and deliver it to them: ... and (wait to) see what answer they return. (The queen) said: Ye chiefs! Here is delivered to me— a letter worthy of respect. It is from Solomon, and is (as follows): In the name of Allah, Most gracious, Most Merciful: Be ye not arrogant against me, but come to me in submission (to the true religion)."[462]

What you read above is not taken from a cartoon, nor is it a quote from a comedy play or comic book; *it was actually and directly quoted from the Qur'an!*

The Qur'an continues, claiming the queen of Sheba declined Solomon's invitation and rejected faith in Islam, but she courteously sent back a gift to Solomon with the hoopoe.

461) Sura *An-Naml* 27:22.
462) Sura *An-Naml* 27:28-31.

However, Solomon got angry at her response, so he gathered the Jinns, the birds, and his counselors, and said to them:

"Ye chiefs, which of you can bring me her throne before they come to me in submission?"[463]

What did his counselors of Jinns, birds, and men respond to his angry demands, according the Qur'an? Do you even *want* to read the rest of Sura 27 to find out? How can anyone with a sound mind believe this story?

---

463) Sura *An-Naml* 27:38.

11

Muslim Rituals

In the courts of this world, a man can be declared guilty if the prosecution presents one single proof for the guilt of the accused. However, in this book, dozens of damning proofs are presented to disprove the claim that the Qur'an is God-sent. These proofs are presented to confirm that Islam is a man-made religion and the Qur'an is a man-made book – not from the God of the Bible.

Now we will examine Islamic rituals. Please note that all these rituals were copied from the Old Testament, with some modifications, so Muslims would have the luxury of saying they were not simply taken from the Bible. Unfortunately, the modifications are enough to distort the true meaning of these supreme rituals. Even some causes behind some of these rituals were distorted, as well.

The rituals Islam adopted are: prayer, fasting, giving of alms, pilgrimage, women's status, the law of marriage, and the teaching about Paradise. We will discuss three: prayer, fasting and pilgrimage. What is the point of view of the Qur'an and Muhammad, the Muslims' Messenger?

Prayer

In the *Hadith* a story attributed to Muhammad says that he went up to heaven and had an audience with Allah. During that audience, Allah commanded both him and the Muslims to pray the Muslim prayer fifty times per day. As he was leaving Allah's presence, he saw Moses, and told him what Allah had commanded him. Moses told Muhammad to go back to Allah and tell him that such a command would be a great burden to his people. Muhammad went in and told Allah what Moses suggested. Allah changed His mind and told Muhammad that they could pray *forty* times per day. Moses, at the door, told Muhammad to go back and bargain with Allah again, which he did. Allah agreed to bring the prayer down to *thirty* times. Moses was not satisfied, so Muhammad had to go back to bring the number down to twenty, then to ten, and finally to five times of prayer per day.[464] The five prayers start at dawn and end two hours after sunset, which is known as the supper prayer.[465]

Before each prayer, the Muslim is required to cleanse himself (*Woodoo'*) by washing up. Purity in Islam is a material, physical cleansing. If the person to pray does not cleanse him or herself, his/her prayer cannot be accepted by Allah. Nothing is said about the spiritual cleansing of the soul.

The most important time of prayer in Islam is the Friday noon prayer, for which Muhammad's god gives the praying person great rewards.

---

464) Notice the similarity between this myth and the true story of Abraham asking God not to destroy Sodom if only 10 righteous were there. See Genesis 18:20-33.
465) See the *Hadith* of Sahih Bukhari, Vol. 1, Book 8, #345; Vol. 4, Book 54, #429; Vol. 5, Book 58, #227; Vol. 9, Book 93, #608; the *Hadith* of Sahih Muslim, Book 1, #309, 313, 314; and the *Sunan Abu-Dawud* Book 1, #247.

There is a story that tells what caused Muhammad's god to grant those rewards. Muhammad was addressing the people in the Mosque at the time of Friday prayer. All of a sudden, the mosque was emptied as he was speaking. All those who were praying rushed out, and Muhammad was left alone at the pulpit. Why did all those who were praying leave the mosque before the prayer meeting was concluded?

In the *Hadith,* the following explanation is given:

"Those who were praying heard that a caravan of camels came from Damascus carrying much merchandise. So, they got up and went to meet that caravan."[466]

There Muhammad found himself in a dilemma, and decided to solve the problem. The first and fastest solution was a verse carried down to him by "Gabriel:"

"But when they see some bargain or some amusement, they disperse headlong to it, and leave thee standing. Say: 'The (blessing) from the Presence of Allah is better than any amusement or bargain! and Allah is the Best to provide (for all needs).'"[467]

The second solution Muhammad came up with was the rewards that Allah would give those who set aside a time to pray at the Mosque on Friday.

What were the rewards Muhammad promised his followers for praying on Friday noon?

Abu Al-Abbas stated that Muhammad said:

---

466) See the *Hadith* of Sahih Muslim, Book 4, Chapter 157, "Concerning the Words of the Qur'an: 'And When They See Merchandise or Sport, They Break Away to It, and Leave Thee Standing' (62:11)," #1877-1881. See also the *Hadith* of Sahih Bukhari, Vol. 3, Book 34, #274 & 278.
467) Sura *Al-Jumu'ah* (the Day of Congregation) 62:11.

"Washing is cleansing (*woodoo'*). Friday would be a day of atonement. Every foot (walking to the Mosque) [please notice the singular 'foot'[468]] will be considered equal to twenty years of good works."

Any person completing the Friday prayer would earn the works of two hundred years. So if someone lived sixty or seventy years, what would be his rewards if he went to the Mosque every Friday of his life? (Remember, every Friday is equal to about twenty years of work.) With Muhammad promising rewards like this, no wonder the mosques are over-crowded with worshippers.[469]

In Islam, prayer is supposed to be done during specific times. أوقات الصلاة اليومية . However, Christian believers can pray at any time, anywhere, without going through any ritual. Prayer in Christianity is not a ritual; it is a part of a personal relationship between man and God the Father and His Son. For this reason, the Bible encourages us to pray at all times.[470] In another place it says, "Pray without ceasing."[471] This is to teach the believers that there is no specific time to meet God.

In Islam, at the specific time of prayer, a person can spread his rug on the side of the road, even in a crowded place and pray, so everyone can see how religious he is. In Christianity, the Lord Jesus orders us:

---

468) See the *Hadith* of Sahih Bukhari, Vol. 1, Book 11, #625.
469) Another story states that for every step taken toward the mosque, one is raised one degree in rewards &/or has one sin taken off his record. See the *Hadith* of Sahih Bukhari, Vol. 1, Book 11, #620; Vol. 3, Book 34, #330; and the *Hadith* of Sahih Muslim, Book 4, #1376 & 1406. A third story says every step is worth one year's praying and fasting. See the *Sunan Abu-Dawud*, Book 1, #345.
470) See Luke 18:1.
471) 1 Thessalonians 5:17.

"And when thou prayest, thou shalt not be as the hypocrites are: for they love to pray standing in the synagogues and in the corners of the streets, that they may be seen by men. Verily I say unto you, They have their reward. But thou, when thou prayest, enter into thy closet, and when thou hast shut thy door, pray to thy Father which is in secret; and thy Father which seeth in secret shall reward thee openly."[472]

The Lord Jesus taught us that prayer is something personal between us and God, not for the world to watch and praise us for our religiosity. The awesomeness of prayer in real Christianity lies in the fact that God is always there to hear our prayers. Jesus Christ taught:

"But when you pray, use not vain repetitions, as the heathen do: for they think that they shall be heard for their much speaking. Be not ye therefore like unto them: for your Father knoweth what things ye have need of, before ye ask Him."[473]

The Washing before Prayer (Woodoo' الوضوء)

The ritual in Islam that is strictly required of Muslim before he prays is the washing. A Muslim is required to wash his face, his hands, his elbows and his feet before he prays so that his prayer can be accepted. But in Arabia, water is very rare. So Muhammad ruled that if Muslims could not find water, they can use sand. But how could sand cleanse the body? The use of sand was suggested by Aisha, and of course it was immediately accepted by "Gabriel," who brought down confirmation as a Qur'anic verse.[474] I guess such a suggestion had its place. What would have happened to the

472) Matthew 6:5-6.
473) Matthew 6:7-8.
474) See *An-Nisa'* (the Women) 4:43.

prayers of all the Muslims in Muslim countries that have a water shortage? *Prayer definitely not accepted.* A big crisis!

What Makes a Muslim's Prayer Unacceptable?

First, Islamic teaching says that Allah does not accept the prayer of anyone who breaks wind while praying until he/she washes again and restarts the prayer. Breaking wind as one prays corrupts the prayer. Therefore Muslim should go back and rewash, then restart his prayer. It's ironic: breaking wind corrupts the prayer, but washing the face, feet and hands with sand, which is really dirt, does not corrupt a prayer, but (according to Aisha and Muhammad's god) cleanses it?

Second, Ibn Hazam, a renowned Muslim scholar, wrote:

"The passing of a donkey, a dog, or a woman in front of man who is praying does corrupt the prayer; and therefore, the person who is praying should repeat it (repeat the washing and the prayer)."[475]

Thus, Islam came to put women on the same level as (and assign the same value as) donkeys and dogs. As a matter of fact, Aisha, the Mother of the Believers, complained once to Muhammad's companions, "You have equaled us to dogs and donkeys." Muhammad taught that to his men, but he did not *dare* mention it in front of Aisha!

On the other hand, Christianity has a different look at women:

"Likewise, ye husbands, dwell with them according to knowledge, giving honor unto the wife, as unto the weaker vessel, and as being heirs together of the grace of life; that your prayers be not hindered."[476]

According to the Islamic faith, the very presence of a

---

475) See *Al-Muhalla* by Ibn Hazam, Vol. IV, pp. 8-11.
476) 1 Peter 3:7.

woman can corrupt the prayer of a man. But in Christianity, a woman is one of the graces of life, who deserves better honor. This subject deserves our attention so we can treat woman with the honor they deserve.

Fasting

The Qur'an says:

"Fasting has been imposed upon you as it was imposed upon those who came before you."[477]

Here, two points about fasting should be understood. In Islam, there is the mandatory fasting that was imposed by the Qur'an, and there is the voluntary Sunna fasting that was suggested by Muhammad, which has its own rewards.

Mandatory Fasting

The mandatory fast is thirty days, unless the moon appears earlier at the end of the month; then it is twenty-nine days. In Arabic, this month of fasting is called the month of Ramadan. It seems to be Muhammad's and his god Allah's most favorable month. During that month, Muslims claim the Qur'an came down upon Muhammad, though Islamic history tells a totally different story. Also during the month of Ramadan they have The Night of Fate. The Qur'an says:

"The Night of Fate is better than one thousand months, in it the angels and the spirit come down…"[478]

Consequently, during that night, Muslims present their requests and supplications to their god, wishing and hoping they will come true. For the one whose wish is granted, it is said that the window of fate was open for him that night, and that Allah answered his prayers. In other words, in the

---

477) Sura *Al-Baqara* (the Cow) 2:183, author's translation.
478) Sura *Al-Qadr* (Fate or Power) 97:3-4, author's translation.

Night of Fate, Allah answers the wishes of a few and denies the answer to most. This makes the Night of Fate like the lottery, where only one in millions wins the grand prize.

Fasting during the month of Ramadan is mandatory. Muslim fasts from everything: eating, drinking and sex. Fasting lasts from sunrise until sunset. In Saudi Arabia, there are men who roam the streets, forcing men to open their mouth to see if there tongues are white, to prove that they are fasting. But if the tongue is pink, then they are brought to the magistrate who orders their flogging. They take the matter of fasting *that* seriously.

As mentioned above, "Fasting has been imposed upon you as it was imposed upon those who came before you." But *who* imposed fasting and *who* are those who came before? Of course, supposedly God imposed fasting. Those who came before supposedly means the Jews and Christians. They are the ones who preceded Islam and the Muslims, and are mentioned as such in many verses in the Qur'an.

As you can see, Muhammad and the Muslims copied the Jews and Christians practice of fasting. The way of Muslim fasting agrees with the Jew's fasting. It also looks like the fasting of the Catholic Church, where they imposed forty days of fasting. However, Muslims fast for thirty days.

The evenings of the month of Ramadan are evenings of celebrating, feasting and much eating. (Americans have two similar days of feasting, Thanksgiving and Christmas.) Muslims have that Thanksgiving-type feasting thirty days in a row during Ramadan. But if you look at a fasting Muslim during the day, he appears gloomy and grouchy because of his empty stomach. Also, because of fasting, energy falls and is an excuse to be lazy during workdays. If one is blamed for his laziness, he will answer, "Excuse me, I am fasting."

After thirty days of fasting comes three days of festivities of the Feast of Al-Fitr. All Muslim countries, over fifty of them, give their citizens three days to celebrate. While celebrating, they complain that the month of Ramadan ended!

Totally unlike this, the Bible says:

> "Moreover, when ye fast, be not as the hypocrites, of sad countenance: for they disfigure their faces, that they may appear unto men to fast. Verily I say unto you, They have their reward. But thou, when thou fastest, anoint thy head, and wash thy face; That thou appear not unto men to fast, but unto thy Father, which is in secret: and thy Father, which seeth in secret, shall reward thee openly."[479]

It is obvious that such words are the words of God: no pretensions, no public demonstrations to let everyone know that you are fasting. Here, fasting is a personal matter between man and God, and no one should know about it. God said that we should wash our faces to look fresh and not pretend that fasting is a hard chore. The one who fasts may not make it a priority to draw the attention, admiration or the sympathy of his friends, neighbors and strangers.

The Pilgrimage to Mecca

Pilgrimage to Mecca is the fourth pillar in the faith of Islam after prayers, fasting and giving of alms. Pilgrimage to Mecca is mandatory for every financially able Muslim. However, many disabled people take this pilgrimage.

The pilgrimage to Mecca is not something Islam brought to Arabia. The pagan Arabian tribes practiced that ritual hundreds of years before Islam. The Jews and Christians of the Arabian Peninsula had *never* made that pilgrimage

---

479) Matthew 6:16-18.

to Mecca. Only idol worshippers did, and Islam made no changes to that pagan practice. The march between the hills As-Safa and Al-Marwah, the walk around the Ka'aba, and the kissing of the black stone, were all pagan rituals and practices observed long before Islam, and comfortably continued, *without any change*, after Islam.

How did the heathens look at the As-Safa and Al-Marwah? What is called As-Safa was in reality, for the Arabian heathens, the idol *Assaf*, but Muhammad renamed it Safa. What is called Al-Marwah, was for the Arabians before Islam, the idol *Na'ila*. Muhammad could change those names to As-Safa and Al-Marwah with the help of his "Gabriel," who was always available to solve his problems.

Initially, Muslims complained, telling Muhammad that such rituals should not be practiced because they were heathen. Muhammad told them that Allah wills that the Muslims make that walk. Consequently, the following verse came down to him from Allah:

> "Behold, Safa and Marwah are among the Symbols [rituals] of Allah. So if those who visit the House [Ka'aba in Mecca] in the season or at other times, should compass them round, it is no sin in them. And if anyone obeyeth his own impulse to good – Be sure that Allah is He Who recognizeth and knoweth."[480]

Muhammad said that the Pilgrimage is *Urfa*, which means that the Muslim pilgrim should stand on Mount Urfa. If he does not do that, his pilgrimage does not count. Also, he should go up to Mount Al-Muzdalafa and Mount Mani'. But what does a spiritual pilgrimage have to do with hopping over some mountains?

---

480) Sura *Al-Baqara* 2:158.

Then, after climbing those mountains, he should throw some stones at the devil. When I went there, I saw women throw their shoes and men use sticks to beat the devil as though he were right there in front of them. I myself heard a woman "beating the devil" with her slipper and cursing at him, saying, "You caused my divorce from my husband, you #@&%!!" Muslims beat on the devil in Mecca, year in, year out. You would think he would have *left* that area by now!

After the Muslim pilgrim finishes all his required walking and climbing, he must go to a barber and shave his hair. The shaving should start on the right side. If it starts on the left side, the whole pilgrimage will not count.

Finally, the pilgrim must offer a lamb as a sacrifice on his behalf. During the days of Muhammad, Muslim pilgrims numbered in the hundreds. But now more than two million attend to the rituals of the pilgrimage at the same time. Every year, this has caused many to die by suffocation, a bridge breaking or a stampede in a tunnel.

The strangest thing about the Islamic pilgrimage is the one that is made *by proxy*, representing disabled or old people. But the pilgrimage can also be made on behalf of dead people who could not make it to Mecca while they were alive. In fact, it was Muhammad himself who permitted such a practice.[481]

Furthermore, Muhammad also permitted people to die for someone who is already dead, or fast for someone who cannot fast or is already dead.[482] All these deeds are considered debts to Allah that should be paid by a volunteer even after a loved one is dead, to secure his rewards in heaven.

---

481) See *Reviewing Al-Fatawi* by Sheikh Mutwalli Al-Sha'rawi, Vol. IV, p. 188; and the *Hadith* of Sahih Bukhari, Vol. 3, Book 29, #77.
482) See the *Hadith* of Sahih Bukhari, Vol. 3, Book 31, #173-174.

What is the purpose of the pilgrimage to boiling Mecca? Does Allah imposes such rituals of hardship because he wants to inflict vengeance upon his creatures?

It is hard to understand why Muhammad's god sends worshippers to perform some walks and climbs that have no spiritual value, especially since the death toll of the pilgrims to Mecca climbs every year.

After one hears what Muhammad said about the rewears for making the pilgrimage to Mecca, one understands why Muslims make the effort to make the pilgrimage. Abd Al-Aziz Al-Shanwi wrote, quoting Ibn Abbas, who quoted Muhammad:

> "The pilgrim who (finishes his pilgrimage) mounting a donkey, will have seventy good deeds for every step the donkey makes. But if he was walking on his feet, he will earn seven hundred good deeds of the Holy House (of the Ka'aba). When he was asked, What is the good deed of the Holy House? He (Muhammad) answered, Every good deed is equal to one hundred thousand (regular) good deeds."[483]

If that were true, then if one walked from his country to Mecca and completed his pilgrimage walking, he would have such a reserve it would wipe out all of his own sins, and all the sins of the whole Muslim world!

The true God is generous and merciful. That is why He arranged to give us eternal life by grace, only through faith, not by works. It seems obvious that he who instituted the pilgrimage rituals thought people are stupid enough to believe such a hoax.

I pray that many of my brethren will realize the truth.

---
483) *Fuqaha' Al-Sahaba* by Abd Al-Aziz Al-Shanwi, p. 117.

12

Suicide Bombers and Paradise

In the last few months the phenomenon of suicide-bombers, in Israel-Palestine, Indonesia, the United States, Germany, Russia, Saudi Arabia, Pakistan, Somalia, Kenya and other countries around the world, is described by many Muslims as a "martyrdom operation." In most cases, if not all, the suicide bombers were Muslims. Ask yourself: why are so many Muslims ready to blow themselves up in such operations? How could the planners of such operations convince those Muslim young men to commit suicide, or as they put it, "to become martyrs"?

For example, In Palestine-Israel (we will not discuss politics in this chapter), Christians constitute 12% of the population. Why has no Christian Palestinian committed the act of suicide bombing? Is not Palestine their country, too? Aren't the Christians encountering the same problems as their Muslim counterparts? Moreover, over 95% of the suicide-bombers are young men, not young women. Why?

Many writers have analyzed the problem but they come up with conflicting answers. Some of them touch on the truth but others are far from it. In this chapter we will enter into the core of the problem and answer this important question: Why would a Muslim so cruelly end his young life at his own hands? Why would he commit merciless murder of the innocent, like the operation of September 11, 2001?

I have found the answer in what Islam teaches about their Paradise. What is the Paradise that the Muslim scholars, quoting their Prophet Muhammad, describe? For them, and in their teachings, Paradise is rivers of wine and milk, palaces, fruit trees, eternally nice looking lads, and the most important in it are the beautiful women. The Qur'an says:

> "(Here is) a parable of the Garden [Paradise] which the righteous are promised: in it are rivers of water incorruptible; rivers of milk of which the taste never changes; rivers of wine, a joy to those who drink; and rivers of honey pure and clear. In it there are for them all kinds of fruits; and grace from their Lord."[484]

The Qur'an gives a detailed description of Paradise:

> "These will be those nearest to Allah in Gardens of bliss: a number of people from those of old, and a few from those of later times. (They will be) on thrones encrusted (with gold and precious stones), reclining on them, facing each other. Round about them will (serve) them youths of perpetual (freshness), with goblets, (shining) beakers, and cups (filled) out of clear-flowing fountains: No after-ache will they receive therefrom, nor will they suffer intoxication: and with fruits, any that they may select; and the flesh of fowls, any that they may desire. And (there will be) [lady] Companions with beautiful, big and lustrous eyes, like unto Pearls well guarded. A re-

---

484) Sura *Muhammad* 47:15.

ward for the deeds of their past (life). No frivolity will they hear therein, nor any taint of ill."[485]

The Qur'an continues its description of Paradise:

"In shade long-extended, by water flowing constantly, and fruit in abundance whose season is not limited, nor (supply) forbidden. And on thrones raised high. We have created (their [female] companions) of special creation, and made them virgin-pure (and undefiled), beloved (by nature), equal in age."[486]

This is the Paradise, with all its enticements, that Allah offers to those who become martyrs for the cause of Islam.

What does Muhammad himself say about Paradise? Before those quotations are cited, the reader is owed an apology for the profane/sexual language that is used by Muhammad in his statements (الحديث). Even after many of the terms are taken out, the language is still embarrassing. Here, Sheikh Al-Sha'rawi quotes Muhammad:

"The Messenger of Allah was asked, Shall we have sex in Paradise; he answered, Yes, in the name of whose hands is my soul, after the man gets up from upon her (a woman he is having sex with), she turns virgin again."[487]

In another place, Muhammad was asked:

"Do the people in Paradise have sex? He answered: With a penis that does not get soft, and a climax that does not stop."

Al-Sha'rawi added on page 148 of his book:

"The Messenger of Allah (Muhammad) said, In the

---

485) Sura *Al-Waqi'ah* (That Which Is Coming) 56:11-25.
486) Sura *Waqi'ah* 56:30-37.
487) *Al-Fatawi* by Sheikh Mutwalli Al-Sha'rawi, p. 36.

name of whom is my soul, a man can have sex with
a hundred women in one day."

Those who want more references on the sayings of Muhammad about sex in Paradise can read the book by Abu
Al-Abbas, *The Women of Paradise*. In that book he uses the
terms, phrases and word-pictures Muhammad uttered, and
makes the reader think he is watching pornography movies.
On page 41 of that book, Muhammad said:

"Each man in heaven will have the sexual power of
one hundred men."

Ibn Abbas described the women of Paradise (many of the
filthy terms and words were avoided):

"Her breast is like those of a young teenager (i.e.,
they did not sag)."

What does Islam teach about the rewards for those who
becomes a martyrs for the cause of Islam? Abu Al-Abbas
wrote that Muhammad said:

"The martyr will marry seventy-two wives who have
beautiful, luscious eyes."

Abu Al-Abbas wished, as all those who wanted to become
martyrs wished, that Allah would give him the privilege to
enjoy the women of Paradise. Abu Al-Abbas continued to
insist that the virgins of Paradise are much better, more luscious and more desired than the widows.

Muhammad said that whenever a martyr enters Paradise,
he will have two beautiful women with beautiful eyes at his
head and his feet, singing for him. He will have excellent
domiciles in the Garden of Eden. But the home of the martyr is a palace of pearls, having seventy houses and seventy
beds. On each bed will be a beautiful wife with luscious eyes.
Abu Al-Abbas wrote:

> "The man of Paradise will marry 500 beautiful women, 4,000 virgins and 8,000 widows. When he will hug each one of them, his hug will last the length of his life on earth."[488]

After reading what Muhammad taught on this subject, one can easily understand the rush of young men to commit that heinous crime of suicide bombing. Many men would like to say farewell to their poverty and misery so they can enter the Paradise Muhammad described... a place where they will have rivers of wine, palaces of pearls and beautiful women.

However, when they enter eternity, they will find that no such paradise exists.

Jesus Christ said:

> "Ye do err, not knowing the scriptures, nor the power of God. For in the resurrection they neither marry, nor are given in marriage, but are as the angels of God in heaven."[489]

God's heaven is holy and pure, not a place for material and sexual lust.

The most disturbing thing about the Paradise of Muhammad is that it is only for men, who "rule the roost" there. Almost nothing exists for women, except pleasing men and fulfilling their sexual desires.

Just a note: Among all suicide-bombers, it is almost impossible to find a Christian who commits that crime. Why? Because Christ told us to love one another, not blow one another up!

Christ taught that Heaven is *holy* and *pure*:

---

488) *The Women of Paradise* by Abu Al-Abbas, Vol. IV.
489) Matthew 22:29-30.

"And there shall in no wise enter into it any thing that defileth, neither whatsoever worketh abomination, or maketh a lie: but they which are written in the Lamb's book of life."[490]

490) Revelation 21:27.

Conclusion

I wrote this book so my Muslim friends and relatives and all Muslims may read the truth and accept it, so the Lord Jesus Christ may accept them into the family of God.

Muslims pray several times a day that Allah will direct them to the Straight Path.[491]

Jesus says:

> "I am the Way, the Truth, and the Life, no man cometh unto the Father but by me."[492]

The Lord Jesus Christ is the straight Path, the Way that will take you to heaven. If you want to reach heaven, you have no choice but to believe that Jesus Christ died to pay for your sins. Accept Him as your Lord and Saviour. Then you will reach that holy and pure heaven, where you will not be disappointed. Amen.

---

491) See Sura *Al-Fatihah* (the Opening) 1:6; *Al-Muzammil* (the Mantled One) 73:19; and *Ad-Dahr (*or *Al-Insan)* (the Man) 76:29.
492) John 14:6.

Appendix A
Suras of the Qur'an

Sura 1 Al-Fatihah (The Opening)
Sura 2 Al-Baqara (The Cow)
Sura 3 Al-Imran (The Family Of Imran)
Sura 4 An-Nisa' (The Women)
Sura 5 Al-Ma'idah (The Table Spread, or The Food)
Sura 6 Al-An'am (The Cattle)
Sura 7 Al-A'raf (The Elevated Places)
Sura 8 Al-Anfal (The Spoils Of War)
Sura 9 At-Tauba (Repentance)
Sura 10 Yunus (Jonah)
Sura 11 Hud
Sura 12 Yusuf (Joseph)
Sura 13 Ar-Ra'd (The Thunder)
Sura 14 Ibrahim (Abraham)
Sura 15 Al-Hijr (The Rock)
Sura 16 An-Nahl (The Bee)
Sura 17 Bani Isra'il (The Israelites)
Sura 18 Al-Kahf (The Cave)
Sura 19 Maryam (Mary)
Sura 20 Ta Ha
Sura 21 Al-Anbiya' (The Prophets)
Sura 22 Al-Hajj (The Pilgrimage)
Sura 23 Al-Mu'minun (The Believers)

Sura 24 An-Nur (The Light)
Sura 25 Al-Furqan (The Criterion)
Sura 26 Ash-Shu'ara' (The Poets)
Sura 27 An-Naml (The Ant)
Sura 28 Al-Qasas (The Narrative)
Sura 29 Al-'Ankabut (The Spider)
Sura 30 Ar-Rum (The Romans)
Sura 31 Luqman (Lukman)
Sura 32 As-Sajdah (The Adoration)
Sura 33 Al-Ahzab (The Allies)
Sura 34 Saba' (Sheba)
Sura 35 Al-Fatir (The Creator)
Sura 36 Ya Sin (Ya Sin)
Sura 37 As-Saffat (The Rangers)
Sura 38 Sad
Sura 39 Az-Zumar (The Crowds)
Sura 40 Al-Mu'min (The Forgiving One)
Sura 41 Ha Mim Sajdah (Revelations Well Expounded)
Sura 42 Ash-Shura (The Counsel)
Sura 43 Az-Zukhruf (The Embellishment)
Sura 44 Ad-Dukhan (The Smoke)
Sura 45 Al-Jathiyah (The Kneeling)
Sura 46 Al-Ahqaf (The Sandhills)
Sura 47 Muhammad
Sura 48 Al-Fath (The Victory)
Sura 49 Al-Hujurat (The Chambers)
Sura 50 Qaf
Sura 51 Adh-Dhariyat (The Scatterers)
Sura 52 At-Tur (The Mountain)
Sura 53 An-Najm (The Star)
Sura 54 Al-Qamar (The Moon)
Sura 55 Ar-Rahman (The Merciful)

Sura 56 Al-Waqi'ah (That Which Is Coming)
Sura 57 Al-Hadid (The Iron)
Sura 58 Al-Mujadilah (She Who Pleaded)
Sura 59 Al-Hashr (The Exile)
Sura 60 Al-Mumtahanah (She Who is Tested)
Sura 61 As-Saff (The Ranks)
Sura 62 Al-Jumu'ah (The Day of Congregation)
Sura 63 Al-Munafiqun (The Hypocrites)
Sura 64 At-Taghabun (The Cheating)
Sura 65 At-Talaq (The Divorce)
Sura 66 At-Tahrim (The Prohibition)
Sura 67 Al-Mulk (The Kingdom)
Sura 68 Al-Qalam (The Pen)
Sura 69 Al-Haqqah (The Inevitable)
Sura 70 Al-Ma'arij (The Ladders)
Sura 71 Nuh (Noah)
Sura 72 Al-Jinn (The Jinn)
Sura 73 Al-Muzammil (The Mantled One)
Sura 74 Al-Mudathir (The Clothed One)
Sura 75 Al-Qiyamah (The Resurrection)
Sura 76 Ad-Dahr (The Man)
Sura 77 Al-Mursalat (The Emissaries)
Sura 78 An-Naba' (The Tidings)
Sura 79 An-Nazi'at (Those Who Pull Out)
Sura 80 'Abasa (He Frowned)
Sura 81 At-Takwir (The Cessation)
Sura 82 Al-Infitar (The Cleaving Asunder)
Sura 83 At-Tatfif (The Defrauders)
Sura 84 Al-Inshiqaq (The Rending)
Sura 85 Al-Buruj (The Constellations)
Sura 86 At-Tariq (The Night-Comer)
Sura 87 Al-A'la (The Most High)

Sura 88 Al-Ghashiya (The Overwhelming Calamity)
Sura 89 Al-Fajr (The Dawn)
Sura 90 Al-Balad (The City)
Sura 91 Ash-Shams (The Sun)
Sura 92 Al-Layl (The Night)
Sura 93 Ad-Duha (The Early Hours)
Sura 94 Al-Inshirah (The Expansion)
Sura 95 At-Tin (The Fig)
Sura 96 Al-'Alaq (The Clot)
Sura 97 Al-Qadr (Fate, Power)
Sura 98 Al-Bayyinah (The Proof)
Sura 99 Al-Zilzal (The Shaking)
Sura 100 Al-'Adiyat (The Assaulters)
Sura 101 Al-Qari'ah (The Terrible Calamity)
Sura 102 At-Takathur (Worldly Gain)
Sura 103 Al-'Asr (Time [through the Ages])
Sura 104 Al-Humazah (The Slanderer)
Sura 105 Al-Fil (The Elephant)
Sura 106 Al-Quraysh (The Quraish)
Sura 107 Al-Ma`un (The Daily Necessaries)
Sura 108 Al-Kauthar (Abundance)
Sura 109 Al-Kafirun (The Unbelievers)
Sura 110 An-Nasr (The Help)
Sura 111 Al-Lahab (The Flame)
Sura 112 Al-Ikhlas (The Unity)
Sura 113 Al-Falaq (The Daybreak)
Sura 114 An-Nas (The Men)
Sura 115 Al-Wilaya (Sura of Succession, only found in Shi'ite Qur'ans)

Appendix B

Subject Index